Doing Business 2020

Comparing Business Regulation in 190 Economies

WORLD BANK GROUP

1818 H Street NW, Washington, DC 20433
Telephone: 202-473-1000; Internet: www.worldbank.org

1 2 3 4 22 21 20 19

ISBN (paper): 978-1-4648-1440-2
ISBN (electronic): 978-1-4648-1441-9
DOI: 10.1596/978-1-4648-1440-2

Cover design: Bill Pragluski, Critical Stages

Library of Congress Control Number: 2019951789

Resources on the *Doing Business* website

Current features
News on the *Doing Business* project
http://www.doingbusiness.org

Rankings
How economies rank—from 1 to 190
http://www.doingbusiness.org/rankings

Data
All the data for 190 economies—topic rankings, indicator values, lists of regulatory procedures and details underlying indicators
http://www.doingbusiness.org/data

Studies
Access to previous editions of *Doing Business* as well as subnational and regional studies, case studies and customized economy and regional profiles
http://www.doingbusiness.org/reports

Methodology
The methodologies and research papers underlying *Doing Business*
http://www.doingbusiness.org/methodology

Research
Abstracts of papers on *Doing Business* topics and related policy issues
http://www.doingbusiness.org/research

Doing Business reforms
Short summaries of DB2020 business regulation reforms and lists of reforms since DB2006
http://www.doingbusiness.org/reforms

Historical data
Customized data sets since DB2004
http://www.doingbusiness.org/custom-query

Law library
Online collection of business laws and regulations relating to business
http://www.doingbusiness.org/law-library

Contributors
More than 15,000 specialists in 190 economies who participate in *Doing Business*
http://www.doingbusiness.org/contributors/doing-business

Entrepreneurship data
Data on new business density (number of newly registered companies per 1,000 working-age people) for 156 economies
http://www.doingbusiness.org/data/exploretopics/entrepreneurship

Ease of doing business score
Data benchmarking 190 economies to the best regulatory practice and an ease of doing business score calculator
https://www.doingbusiness.org/data/doing-business-score

Contents

- *Doing Business 2020* is the 17th in a series of annual studies investigating the regulations that enhance business activity and those that constrain it. *Doing Business* presents quantitative indicators on business regulations and the protection of property rights that can be compared across 190 economies—from Afghanistan to Zimbabwe—and over time.
- Regulations affecting 12 areas of the life of a business are covered: starting a business, dealing with construction permits, getting electricity, registering property, getting credit, protecting minority investors, paying taxes, trading across borders, enforcing contracts, resolving insolvency, employing workers, and contracting with the government. The employing workers and contracting with the government indicator sets are not included in this year's ranking on the ease of doing business.
- Data in *Doing Business 2020* are current as of May 1, 2019. The indicators are used to analyze economic outcomes and identify what reforms of business regulation have worked, where and why.

Foreword

The *Doing Business 2020* study shows that developing economies are catching up with developed economies in ease of doing business.

Still, the gap remains wide. An entrepreneur in a low-income economy typically spends around 50 percent of the country's per-capita income to launch a company, compared with just 4.2 percent for an entrepreneur in a high-income economy. It takes nearly six times as long on average to start a business in the economies ranked in the bottom 50 as in the top 20.

There's ample room for developing economies to catch up with developed countries on most of the *Doing Business* indicators. Performance in the area of legal rights, for example, remains weakest among low- and middle-income economies.

Doing Business recognizes the important work countries have done to improve their regulatory environments. Among the 10 economies that advanced the most, efforts were focused on the areas of starting a business, dealing with construction permits, and trading across borders. In general, economies that score the highest share several features, including the widespread use of electronic systems and online platforms to comply with regulatory requirements.

At the same time, the least reformed area was resolving insolvency. Putting in place reorganization procedures reduces the failure rates of small and medium-size enterprises and prevents the liquidation of insolvent but viable businesses.

Doing Business is a valuable tool that governments can use to design sound regulatory policies. By giving policymakers a way to benchmark progress, it stimulates policy debate, both by exposing potential challenges and by identifying good practices and lessons learned.

It's important to note that *Doing Business* isn't meant to be an investment guide, but rather a measurement of ease of doing business. Potential investors consider many other factors, such as the overall quality of an economy's business environment and its national competitiveness, macroeconomic stability, development of the financial system, market size, rule of law, and the quality of the labor force.

Ease of doing business is an important springboard to structural reforms that encourage broad-based growth. The World Bank Group stands ready to help countries move forward.

David R. Malpass
President
The World Bank Group

Acknowledgments

Data collection and analysis for *Doing Business 2020* were conducted by a team led by Santiago Croci (Program Manager, *Doing Business*) under the general direction of Rita Ramalho (Senior Manager, Global Indicators Group, Development Economics). Overall guidance for the preparation of the study was provided by Simeon Djankov (Senior Director, Development Economics). The project was managed with the support of Adrian Gonzalez, Charlotte Nan Jiang, Valentina Saltane, and Hulya Ulku. Other team members included Marwa Abdou, Youmna Al Hourani, Lucia Arnal Rodriguez, Yuriy Valentinovich Avramov, Ogma Dessirama Bale, Elodie Bataille, Farihane Ben Yedder, Erica Bosio, Liliya F Bulgakova, Kamal Chakaroun, Édgar Chávez, Maria-Magdalena Chiquier, Cyriane Marie Coste, Sabrina Fantoni Custodio, Najah Nina Dannaoui, Theophile de Saint Sernin, Marie Lily Delion, Nadine DiMonte, Varun Eknath, Viktoriya Ereshchenko, Vanessa Maria Cervello Ferrando, Dorina Peteva Georgieva, Claudia Gonzalez Cobos, Tom Kairuz Harb, Becem Hassen, Maho Hatayama, Maksym Iavorskyi, Amina Naomi Idris, Hervé Kaddoura, New Doe Kaledzi, Klaus Koch-Saldarriaga, Olga Kuzmina, Sarah Kouhlani Nolla, Iryna Lagodna, Loic Sebastien Lanci, Anouk Leger, Joseph Lemoine, Tiziana Londero, Silvia Carolina Lopez Rocha, Courtney Masters, Raman Maroz, Rumbidzai Maweni, Margherita Mellone, Nuno Filipe Mendes Dos Santos, Frederic Meunier, Joanna Nasr, Marie-Jeanne Ndiaye, Albert Nogués i Comas, Nadia Novik, Esperanza Pastor Núñez de Castro, Adjoua Marie-Pascale Nzi, Enrique Orellana Tamez, Alexia Pimbli, Marion Pinto, Greta Polo, Oleksandra Popova, Maria Antonia Quesada Gámez, Parvina Rakhimova, Mariyam Raziyeva, Nathalie Reyes Benjumea, Martin Ruiz-Cantu, Julie Anne Ryan, Syuzanna Simonyan, Katarzyna Sokal, Ines Sosa, Jayashree Srinivasan, Mihaela Stangu, Erick Tjong, Judith Trasancos Rodríguez, Farrukh Umarov, Yulia Borisovna Valerio, Rongpeng (Tiffany) Yang, Marilyne Youbi, Inés Zabalbeitia Múgica, Yasmin Zand, Dou Zhang, and Muqiao (Chloe) Zhang.

Yaser Abdulrahman H Alhusaini, Meshal Abdulaziz Alkhowaiter, Daad Abdullah Alshabanah, Adnane Ayeb, Tomilehin Folake Babafemi, Tsenguunjav Byambasuren, Maria Alejandra Castellanos Chavarria, Marie Jose Anne Caroline Chatelain, Maxime Delavallee, Ava Josyane Armande Drai, Shoola Dzhumaeva, Nadine Khaled Eloseily, Caleb Enrique Espinoza, Jade Christian Hachem, Ritika Narayan Iyer, Guyu Jiang, Zan Jin, Clemens Mathis Henrik Graf von Luckner, Daniel Anselmo Marechal, Morris J.

McGinn, Kensi Poukouta, Carolina Nugnes, Ngozi Joann Nwanta, Alexandre Fujishima Silveira de Oliveira, Lodovico Onofri, Lidia Panarello, Manisha Panda, Michele Franchetti Pardo, Roxane Louise Manijeh Peloux, Ziyue Qiu, Hyung Sub Roh, Lukshmee Saravanapavan, Bit Na Ra Shin, Kimberly Suárez-Contreras, Lluis Dalmau Taules, and Qunrui Zhou, assisted in the months before publication.

The team is grateful for the valuable comments provided by colleagues, both within and outside the World Bank Group, and for the guidance provided by World Bank Group Executive Directors.

OVERVIEW

Tackling burdensome regulation

- Worldwide, 115 economies made it easier to do business.
- The economies with the most notable improvement in *Doing Business 2020* are Saudi Arabia, Jordan, Togo, Bahrain, Tajikistan, Pakistan, Kuwait, China, India, and Nigeria.
- Only two African economies rank in the top 50 on the ease of doing business; no Latin American economies rank in this group.

At its core, regulation is about freedom to do business. Regulation aims to prevent worker mistreatment by greedy employers (regulation of labor), to ensure that roads and bridges do not collapse (regulation of public procurement), and to protect one's investments (minority shareholder protections). All too often, however, regulation misses its goal, and one inefficiency replaces another, especially in the form of government overreach in business activity. Governments in many economies adopt or maintain regulation that burdens entrepreneurs. Whether by intent or ignorance, such regulation limits entrepreneurs' ability to freely operate a private business. As a result, entrepreneurs resort to informal activity, away from the oversight of regulators and tax collectors, or seek opportunities abroad—or join the ranks of the unemployed. Foreign investors avoid economies that use regulation to manipulate the private sector.

By documenting changes in regulation in 12 areas of business activity in 190 economies, *Doing Business* analyzes regulation that encourages efficiency and supports freedom to do business.[1] The data collected by *Doing Business* address three questions about government. First, when do governments change regulation with a view to develop their private sector? Second, what are the characteristics of reformist governments? Third, what are the effects of regulatory change on different aspects of economic or investment activity? Answering these questions adds to our knowledge of development.

With these objectives at hand, *Doing Business* measures the processes for business incorporation, getting a building permit, obtaining an electricity connection, transferring property, getting access to credit, protecting minority investors, paying taxes, engaging in international trade, enforcing contracts, and resolving insolvency. *Doing Business* also collects and publishes data on regulation of employment as well as contracting with the government (figure O.1). The employing workers indicator set measures regulation in the areas of hiring, working hours, and redundancy. The contracting with the government indicators capture the time and procedures involved in a standardized public procurement for road resurfacing. These two indicator sets do not constitute part of the ease of doing business ranking.

Research demonstrates a causal relationship between economic freedom and gross domestic product (GDP) growth, where freedom regarding wages and prices, property rights, and licensing requirements leads to economic development.[2] Of the 190 economies measured by *Doing Business 2020*, land registries in 146 lack full geographic coverage of privately owned land. All privately held land plots are formally registered in only 3% of low-income economies. Overall, on the registering property indicator set, 92 economies receive a score of zero on the geographic coverage of privately owned land index, 12 on the transparency of information index, and 31 on the reliability of infrastructure index. Globally, property registration processes remain most inefficient in the South Asia and Sub-Saharan Africa regions.

Doing Business 2020 shows that effectiveness of trading across borders also varies significantly from economy to economy. Economies that

FIGURE O.1 What is measured in *Doing Business*?

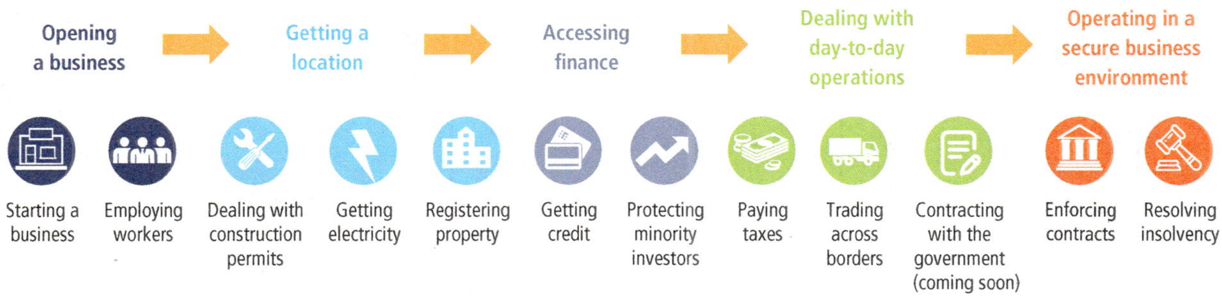

Note: The employing workers and contracting with the government indicator sets are not included in the ease of doing business ranking.

predominantly trade through seaports incur average export border compliance costs as high as $2,223 per shipment in the Democratic Republic of Congo and $1,633 in Gabon compared to only $354 in Benin and $303 in Mauritius. Similarly, documentary compliance costs surge to $1,800 in Iraq, $725 in the Syrian Arab Republic, and $550 in The Bahamas. It is important to note, however, that high costs in Iraq and Syria are also attributed to fragile political, social, and economic conditions. Export border compliance times for maritime transport range from 10 hours in Singapore to over 200 hours in Cameroon and Côte d'Ivoire. According to *Doing Business 2020* data, ports are most efficient in Organisation for Economic Co-operation and Development (OECD) high-income economies and least efficient in Sub-Saharan Africa. Substantial further reform efforts are warranted to spread efficiency to economies where businesses still struggle to trade.

Business regulation: Benchmarking

Doing Business benchmarks aspects of business regulation and practice using specific case studies with standardized assumptions. The strength of the business environment is scored on the basis of an economy's performance in each of the 10 areas included in the ease of doing business ranking (table O.1). This approach facilitates the comparison of regulation across economies. The ease of doing business score serves as the basis for ranking economies on their business environment: the ranking is obtained by sorting the economies by their scores. The ease of doing business score shows an economy's absolute position relative to the best regulatory performance, whereas the ease of doing business ranking is an indication of an economy's position relative to that of other economies.

Doing Business 2020 acknowledges 22 reforms in the 20 top-ranking economies. Since 2003/04, the 20 best-performing economies have carried out a total of 464 regulatory changes, suggesting that even the gold

TABLE 0.1 Ease of doing business ranking

Rank	Economy	DB score	Rank	Economy	DB score	Rank	Economy	DB score
1	New Zealand	*86.8*	65	Puerto Rico (U.S.)	*70.1*	128	Barbados	*57.9*
2	Singapore	*86.2*	66	Brunei Darussalam	*70.1*	129	Ecuador	*57.7*
3	Hong Kong SAR, China	*85.3*	67	Colombia	*70.1*	130	St. Vincent and the Grenadines	*57.1*
4	Denmark	*85.3*	68	Oman	*70.0*	131	Nigeria	*56.9*
5	Korea, Rep.	*84.0*	69	Uzbekistan	*69.9*	132	Niger	*56.8*
6	United States	*84.0*	70	Vietnam	*69.8*	133	Honduras	*56.3*
7	Georgia	*83.7*	71	Jamaica	*69.7*	134	Guyana	*55.5*
8	United Kingdom	*83.5*	72	Luxembourg	*69.6*	135	Belize	*55.5*
9	Norway	*82.6*	73	Indonesia	*69.6*	136	Solomon Islands	*55.3*
10	Sweden	*82.0*	74	Costa Rica	*69.2*	137	Cabo Verde	*55.0*
11	Lithuania	*81.6*	75	Jordan	*69.0*	138	Mozambique	*55.0*
12	Malaysia	*81.5*	76	Peru	*68.7*	139	St. Kitts and Nevis	*54.6*
13	Mauritius	*81.5*	77	Qatar	*68.7*	140	Zimbabwe	*54.5*
14	Australia	*81.2*	78	Tunisia	*68.7*	141	Tanzania	*54.5*
15	Taiwan, China	*80.9*	79	Greece	*68.4*	142	Nicaragua	*54.4*
16	United Arab Emirates	*80.9*	80	Kyrgyz Republic	*67.8*	143	Lebanon	*54.3*
17	North Macedonia	*80.7*	81	Mongolia	*67.8*	144	Cambodia	*53.8*
18	Estonia	*80.6*	82	Albania	*67.7*	145	Palau	*53.7*
19	Latvia	*80.3*	83	Kuwait	*67.4*	146	Grenada	*53.4*
20	Finland	*80.2*	84	South Africa	*67.0*	147	Maldives	*53.3*
21	Thailand	*80.1*	85	Zambia	*66.9*	148	Mali	*52.9*
22	Germany	*79.7*	86	Panama	*66.6*	149	Benin	*52.4*
23	Canada	*79.6*	87	Botswana	*66.2*	150	Bolivia	*51.7*
24	Ireland	*79.6*	88	Malta	*66.1*	151	Burkina Faso	*51.4*
25	Kazakhstan	*79.6*	89	Bhutan	*66.0*	152	Mauritania	*51.1*
26	Iceland	*79.0*	90	Bosnia and Herzegovina	*65.4*	153	Marshall Islands	*50.9*
27	Austria	*78.7*	91	El Salvador	*65.3*	154	Lao PDR	*50.8*
28	Russian Federation	*78.2*	92	San Marino	*64.2*	155	Gambia, The	*50.3*
29	Japan	*78.0*	93	St. Lucia	*63.7*	156	Guinea	*49.4*
30	Spain	*77.9*	94	Nepal	*63.2*	157	Algeria	*48.6*
31	China	*77.9*	95	Philippines	*62.8*	158	Micronesia, Fed. Sts.	*48.1*
32	France	*76.8*	96	Guatemala	*62.6*	159	Ethiopia	*48.0*
33	Turkey	*76.8*	97	Togo	*62.3*	160	Comoros	*47.9*
34	Azerbaijan	*76.7*	98	Samoa	*62.1*	161	Madagascar	*47.7*
35	Israel	*76.7*	99	Sri Lanka	*61.8*	162	Suriname	*47.5*
36	Switzerland	*76.6*	100	Seychelles	*61.7*	163	Sierra Leone	*47.5*
37	Slovenia	*76.5*	101	Uruguay	*61.5*	164	Kiribati	*46.9*
38	Rwanda	*76.5*	102	Fiji	*61.5*	165	Myanmar	*46.8*
39	Portugal	*76.5*	103	Tonga	*61.4*	166	Burundi	*46.8*
40	Poland	*76.4*	104	Namibia	*61.4*	167	Cameroon	*46.1*
41	Czech Republic	*76.3*	105	Trinidad and Tobago	*61.3*	168	Bangladesh	*45.0*
42	Netherlands	*76.1*	106	Tajikistan	*61.3*	169	Gabon	*45.0*
43	Bahrain	*76.0*	107	Vanuatu	*61.1*	170	São Tomé and Príncipe	*45.0*
44	Serbia	*75.7*	108	Pakistan	*61.0*	171	Sudan	*44.8*
45	Slovak Republic	*75.6*	109	Malawi	*60.9*	172	Iraq	*44.7*
46	Belgium	*75.0*	110	Côte d'Ivoire	*60.7*	173	Afghanistan	*44.1*
47	Armenia	*74.5*	111	Dominica	*60.5*	174	Guinea-Bissau	*43.2*
48	Moldova	*74.4*	112	Djibouti	*60.5*	175	Liberia	*43.2*
49	Belarus	*74.3*	113	Antigua and Barbuda	*60.3*	176	Syrian Arab Republic	*42.0*
50	Montenegro	*73.8*	114	Egypt, Arab Rep.	*60.1*	177	Angola	*41.3*
51	Croatia	*73.6*	115	Dominican Republic	*60.0*	178	Equatorial Guinea	*41.1*
52	Hungary	*73.4*	116	Uganda	*60.0*	179	Haiti	*40.7*
53	Morocco	*73.4*	117	West Bank and Gaza	*60.0*	180	Congo, Rep.	*39.5*
54	Cyprus	*73.4*	118	Ghana	*60.0*	181	Timor-Leste	*39.4*
55	Romania	*73.3*	119	Bahamas, The	*59.9*	182	Chad	*36.9*
56	Kenya	*73.2*	120	Papua New Guinea	*59.8*	183	Congo, Dem. Rep.	*36.2*
57	Kosovo	*73.2*	121	Eswatini	*59.5*	184	Central African Republic	*35.6*
58	Italy	*72.9*	122	Lesotho	*59.4*	185	South Sudan	*34.6*
59	Chile	*72.6*	123	Senegal	*59.3*	186	Libya	*32.7*
60	Mexico	*72.4*	124	Brazil	*59.1*	187	Yemen, Rep.	*31.8*
61	Bulgaria	*72.0*	125	Paraguay	*59.1*	188	Venezuela, RB	*30.2*
62	Saudi Arabia	*71.6*	126	Argentina	*59.0*	189	Eritrea	*21.6*
63	India	*71.0*	127	Iran, Islamic Rep.	*58.5*	190	Somalia	*20.0*
64	Ukraine	*70.2*						

Source: Doing Business database.

Note: The rankings are benchmarked to May 1, 2019, and based on the average of each economy's ease of doing business scores for the 10 topics included in the aggregate ranking. For the economies for which the data cover two cities, scores are a population-weighted average for the two cities. Rankings are calculated on the basis of the unrounded scores, while scores with only one digit are displayed in the table.

standard setters have room to improve their business climates. More than half of the economies in the top-20 cohort are from the OECD high-income group; however, the top-20 list also includes four economies from East Asia and the Pacific, two from Europe and Central Asia, as well as one from the Middle East and North Africa and one from Sub-Saharan Africa. Conversely, most economies (12) in the bottom 20 are from the Sub-Saharan Africa region.

Encouragingly, several of the lowest-ranked economies are actively reforming in pursuit of a better business environment. Over the past year, Myanmar introduced substantial improvements in five areas measured by *Doing Business*—starting a business, dealing with construction permits, registering property, protecting minority investors, and enforcing contracts. This ambitious reform program allowed the country to rise out of the bottom 20 to a ranking of 165. In contrast to the economies ranked in the top 20, however, the bottom 20 implemented only 10 reforms in 2018/19.

Economies that score highest on the ease of doing business share several common features, including the widespread use of electronic systems. All of the 20 top-ranking economies have online business incorporation processes, have electronic tax filing platforms, and allow online procedures related to property transfers. Moreover, 11 economies have electronic procedures for construction permitting. In general, the 20 top performers have sound business regulation with a high degree of transparency. The average scores of these economies are 12.2 (out of 15) on the building quality control index, 7.2 (out of 8) on the reliability of supply and transparency of tariffs index, 24.8 (out of 30) on the quality of land administration index, and 13.2 (out of 18) on the quality of judicial processes index. Fourteen of the 20 top performers have a unified collateral registry, and 14 allow a viable business to continue operating as a going concern during insolvency proceedings.

The difference in an entrepreneur's experience in top- and bottom-performing economies is discernible in almost all *Doing Business* topics. For example, it takes nearly six times longer on average to start a business in the economies ranked in the bottom 50 than it does in the top 20. Transferring property in the 20 top economies requires less than two weeks, compared to about three months in the bottom 50. Obtaining an electricity connection in an average bottom-50 economy takes twice the time that it takes in an average top-20 economy; the cost of such a connection is 44 times higher when expressed as a share of income per capita. Also, commercial dispute resolution lasts about 2.1 years in economies ranking in the bottom 50 compared to 1.1 years in the top 20. Notable differences between stronger and weaker performing economies are also evident in the quality of regulation and information. In the top 20, 83% of the adult population on average is covered by either a credit bureau or registry, whereas in the bottom 50 the average coverage is only at 10%.

What do *Doing Business 2020* data show?

When low-income economies achieve higher levels of economic efficiency, they tend to reduce the income gap with more developed ones. One study quantifies the relationship between the regulation of entry and the income gap between developing countries and the United States. It shows that substantial barriers to entry in developing economies account for almost half of the income gap with the United States.[3] These barriers prevent growth and result in persistent poverty. Encouragingly, *Doing Business 2020* continues to show a steady convergence between developing and developed economies, especially in the area of business incorporation (figure O.2). Since 2003/04, 178 economies have implemented 722 reforms captured by the starting a business indicator set, either reducing or eliminating barriers to entry. In all, 106 economies eliminated or reduced minimum capital requirements, about 80 introduced or improved one-stop shops, and more than 160 simplified preregistration and registration formalities. More remains to be done, however.

Despite this convergence, *Doing Business 2020* data suggest that a considerable disparity persists between low- and high-income economies on the ease of starting a business. An entrepreneur in a low-income economy typically spends about 50.0% of income per capita to launch a company, compared to just 4.2% for an entrepreneur in a high-income economy.

FIGURE O.2 The cost of starting a business has fallen over time in developing economies

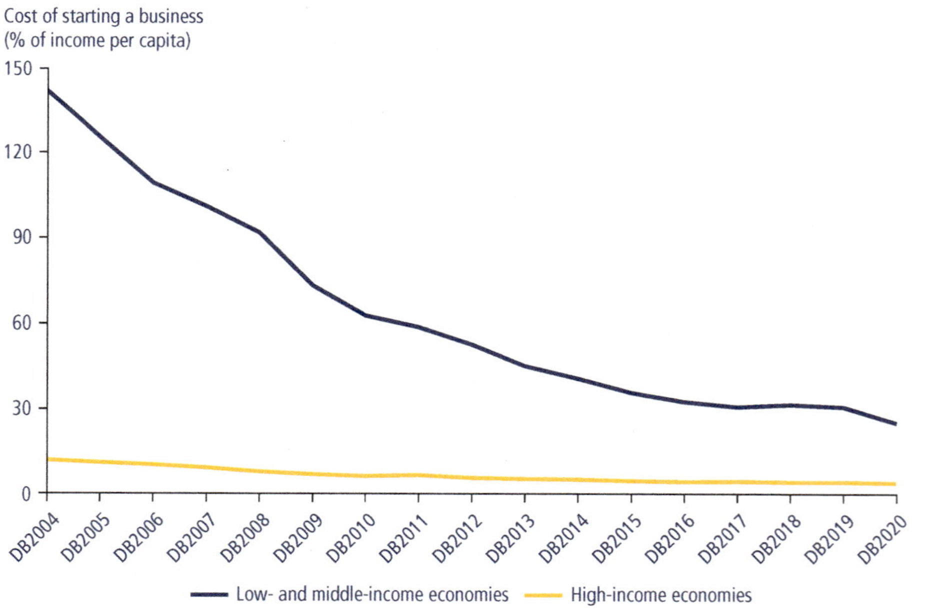

Source: Doing Business database.
Note: The sample comprises 145 economies.

Moreover, the convergence trend does not hold for minimum capital requirements. About one-third of low- and lower-middle-income economies require businesses to set aside a certain amount of minimum capital in addition to regular company incorporation costs. Similarly, the minimum capital requirement is prevalent in one-third of high-income economies.[4]

Ample room still exists for closing the gap between developed and developing economies on most of the *Doing Business* indicators. Performance on the strength of legal rights index, captured by the getting credit indicator set, is weakest among low- and middle-income economies. Credit registries and bureaus in developing economies also tend to collect less comprehensive information with comparatively low coverage, thereby limiting businesses' access to credit. The average credit registry coverage of the adult population in low-income economies is less than 3%, compared to over 22% in high-income ones. Similarly, the average time to meet tax filing obligations is significantly higher in low-income economies (275 hours) than in high-income ones (149 hours). The regions with the most cumbersome tax compliance processes remain Latin America and the Caribbean and Sub-Saharan Africa.

Economies that score well in *Doing Business* benefit from higher levels of entrepreneurial activity (figure O.3). Increased entrepreneurship generates better employment opportunities, higher government tax revenues, and improved personal incomes.

FIGURE O.3 Greater ease of doing business is associated with higher levels of entrepreneurship

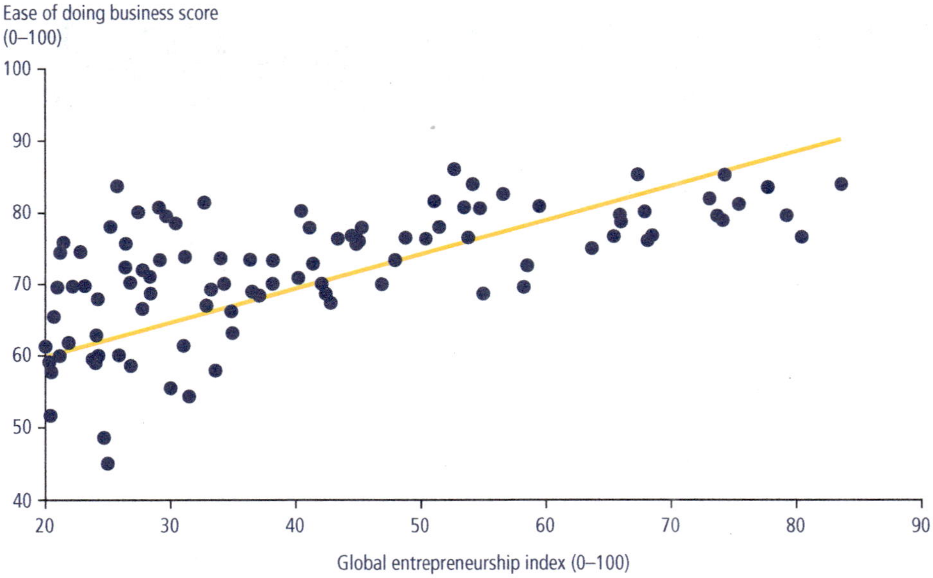

Sources: Doing Business database; Global Entrepreneurship and Development Institute.

Note: The relationship is significant at the 1% level after controlling for income per capita. The sample comprises 135 economies.

Although *Doing Business* does not capture corruption and bribery directly, inefficient regulation tends to go hand in hand with rent-seeking. There are ample opportunities for corruption in economies where excessive red tape and extensive interactions between private sector actors and regulatory agencies are necessary to get things done. The 20 worst-scoring economies on Transparency International's Corruption Perceptions Index average 8 procedures to start a business and 15 to obtain a building permit.[5] Conversely, the 20 best-performing economies complete the same formalities with 4 and 11 steps, respectively. Moreover, economies that have adopted electronic means of compliance with regulatory requirements—such as obtaining licenses and paying taxes—experience a lower incidence of bribery.

Reforming for economic advancement

Doing Business acknowledges the 10 economies that improved the most on the ease of doing business after implementing regulatory reforms.[6] In *Doing Business 2020*, the 10 top improvers are Saudi Arabia, Jordan, Togo, Bahrain, Tajikistan, Pakistan, Kuwait, China, India, and Nigeria (table O.2). These economies implemented a total of 59 regulatory reforms in 2018/19—accounting for one-fifth of all the reforms recorded worldwide. Their efforts focused primarily on the areas of starting a business, dealing with construction permits, and trading across borders.

TABLE O.2 The 10 economies improving the most across three or more areas measured by *Doing Business* in 2018/19

			Reforms making it easier to do business									
Economy	Rank	Change in DB score	Starting a business	Dealing with construction permits	Getting electricity	Registering property	Getting credit	Protecting minority investors	Paying taxes	Trading across borders	Enforcing contracts	Resolving insolvency
Saudi Arabia	62	7.7	✔	✔	✔		✔	✔		✔	✔	✔
Jordan	75	7.6					✔		✔			✔
Togo	97	7.0	✔	✔	✔	✔	✔					
Bahrain	43	5.9		✔	✔	✔	✔	✔	✔	✔	✔	✔
Tajikistan	106	5.7	✔				✔			✔		
Pakistan	108	5.6	✔	✔	✔	✔			✔	✔		
Kuwait	83	4.7	✔	✔	✔	✔	✔	✔		✔		
China	31	4.0	✔	✔	✔			✔	✔	✔	✔	✔
India	63	3.5	✔	✔						✔		✔
Nigeria	131	3.4	✔	✔	✔	✔				✔	✔	

Source: Doing Business database.

Note: See endnote 6 for details on how the top 10 improved economies are assessed.

Jordan and Kuwait are new additions to the list of 10 most improved economies. Nigeria appears as one of the top-10 improvers for the second time. India, which has conducted a remarkable reform effort, joins the list for the third year in a row. Previously, only Burundi, Colombia, the Arab Republic of Egypt, and Georgia featured on the list of 10 top improvers for three consecutive *Doing Business* cycles. Given the size of India's economy, these reform efforts are particularly commendable.

Bahrain implemented the highest number of regulatory reforms (nine), improving in almost every area measured by *Doing Business*.[7] China and Saudi Arabia follow Bahrain with eight reforms each.

One may wonder what underlying factors drive economies to reform. The drivers can be either political or economic or both. The economic advancement of neighboring countries is also an important motivational factor. Research on the effects of market-liberalizing reforms in 144 economies over the period 1995–2006 finds that the most important factor in transmitting reforms between countries is their geographical and cultural proximity. The spillover effect is magnified when more countries adopt reforms that boost economic development. Furthermore, mass media coverage affects political decisions. A recent study finds that economies with higher media coverage of *Doing Business* tend to carry out more business regulatory reforms, with one- and two-year lags between media coverage and reform implementation.[8]

Business regulatory reforms across the Gulf economies have been on a steady rise. These changes are motivated in part by the urgent need for economic diversification. Successful reforms in neighboring states, such as the United Arab Emirates, have also served as inspiration. Saudi Arabia is the most improved economy in *Doing Business 2020*, with a total of eight reforms. With a reformist mindset, the crown prince has implemented and promoted a policy of featuring the Kingdom as an open world-class investment destination. The Kingdom's "Vision 2030" plan for long-term development encompasses a variety of legal and structural reforms.

Pakistan, another top improver, developed an ambitious reform strategy, setting up a national secretariat as well as a prime minister's reform steering committee to ensure progress. Most of the programmed reforms evolved around the *Doing Business* indicators. *Doing Business* working groups have been set up at both municipal and provincial levels.

The motivation for reform in Nigeria, Tajikistan, and Togo was in part the developmental achievements of their neighbors. Rwanda's progress over the past 10 years inspired authorities in Togo, leading several Togolese delegations to visit Kigali to learn about successful reforms. Togo's president set a goal to be number one in West Africa in *Doing Business 2020*. To achieve this target, Togo made significant reform efforts in the areas of starting a business, registering property, and getting credit. Similarly, after observing an economic transformation in neighboring Uzbekistan, Tajikistan's president took a special interest in improving the country's ranking on the ease of doing business.

Nigeria has embarked on a comprehensive reform journey following the example of Kenya.

As in other economies on the list of 10 top improvers, leaders of India and China adopted the *Doing Business* indicators as a core component of their reform strategies. Prime Minister Narendra Modi's "Make in India" campaign focused on attracting foreign investment, boosting the private sector—manufacturing in particular—and enhancing the country's overall competitiveness. The government turned to the *Doing Business* indicators to show investors India's commitment to reform and to demonstrate tangible progress. In 2015 the government's goal was to join the 50 top economies on the ease of doing business ranking by 2020. The administration's reform efforts targeted all of the areas measured by *Doing Business,* with a focus on paying taxes, trading across borders, and resolving insolvency. The country has made a substantial leap upward, raising its ease of doing business ranking from 130 in *Doing Business 2016* to 63 in *Doing Business 2020.*

In recent years China has shown eagerness to reform in the areas captured by *Doing Business*. Chinese Premier Li Keqiang's March 2018 "Report on the Work of the Government" set the stage for municipal governments to implement a reform agenda. The use of *Doing Business* as a benchmark aligns with the central government's ambition to improve the competitiveness of the Chinese economy. The Chinese government also created working groups targeting each of the *Doing Business* indicators. To date, China has shown a notable improvement in the areas of dealing with construction permits (figure O.4), getting electricity, and resolving insolvency.

FIGURE O.4 China has substantially improved the process to obtain a construction permit

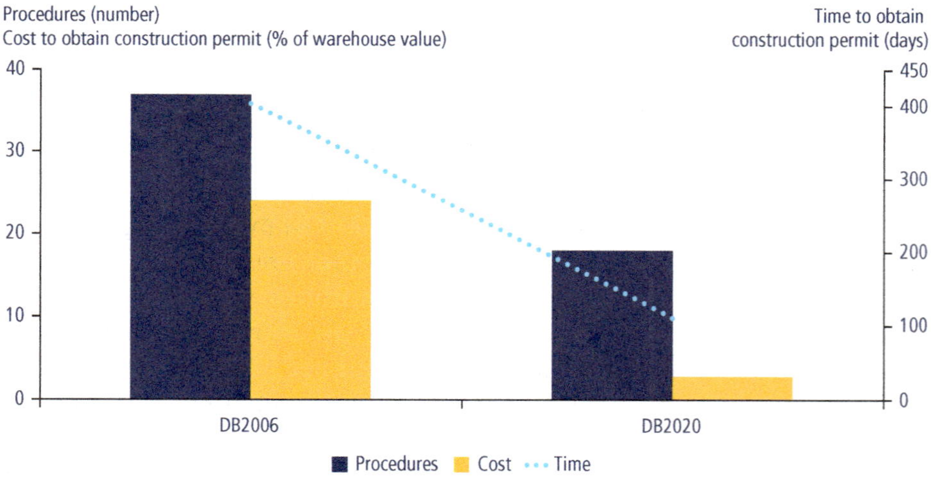

Source: Doing Business database.

What have economies achieved, and who falls behind?

In 2018/19, 115 economies implemented 294 business regulatory reforms across the 10 areas measured by *Doing Business*. Most of these reforms addressed aspects of starting a business, dealing with construction permits, getting electricity, and paying taxes; the least reformed area was resolving insolvency. The most common reform features included advancing the functionality of credit bureaus and registries, developing or enhancing online platforms to comply with regulatory requirements, improving the reliability of power supply, reducing certain taxes, strengthening minority investor protections, streamlining property registration processes, and automating international trade logistics. Low-income economies accounted for 11% of all the regulatory changes, with Togo implementing the highest number of reforms (five).

In Sub-Saharan Africa, Togo represents a bright spot. Sub-Saharan Africa remains one of the weak-performing regions on the ease of doing business with an average score of 51.8, well below the OECD high-income economy average of 78.4 and the global average of 63.0. Compared to the previous year, Sub-Saharan African economies raised their average ease of doing business score by just 1 percentage point in *Doing Business 2020,* whereas economies in the Middle East and North Africa region raised their average score by 1.9.

Latin America and the Caribbean also lags in terms of reform implementation and impact. No economies from this region appeared in the 10 top improvers list over the past two years. Moreover, not a single economy in Latin America and the Caribbean ranks among the top 50 on the ease of doing business. The regional leader on the ease of doing business score, Mexico, is still almost 12 percentage points below the average score of the 10 top-ranking economies.

Globally reforms in the areas of dealing with construction permits and getting electricity have risen sharply in recent years, peaking in 2018/19 at 37 and 34, respectively. Twenty-one of the 37 economies reforming aspects of dealing with construction permits simplified the permitting processes by streamlining interactions with agencies for preapprovals and inspections. Another 16 reformed their building quality control systems. In addition, 12 economies either set up or improved online platforms for processing building permits, and 3 economies launched one-stop shops.

In the area of getting electricity, several Caribbean countries, including Barbados and Belize, invested in training utility personnel and capacity building. In West Africa, Ghana and Nigeria reduced electricity connection times. Sixteen economies made substantial investments in modernizing electric infrastructure through the installation of substations and remote-control systems; others improved distribution network maintenance. Mainly owing to targeted improvements in electricity supply, the average global duration of power cuts fell by 8.3% between 2017 and 2018. Although blackouts remain relatively frequent in Sub-Saharan Africa, utilities in this region made substantial progress in providing a better power supply to their customers.

In 2018/19, 24 economies increased the efficiency of property transfers and improved the quality of land administration. The most common features of property registration reform included greater transparency of information, better reliability of infrastructure, and reduced taxes and fees. Across regions, economies in the Middle East and North Africa improved the most. Qatar created a one-stop shop, eliminating five procedures and lowering property transfer time by 11 days. In Latin America and the Caribbean, Jamaica reduced the cost of property registration by almost 7% of the property value. Brazil and Ecuador introduced electronic property transfer systems.

Thirty economies pursued reforms facilitating firms' access to credit. Five reformers either created unified and functional systems for secured transactions or expanded the scope of movable assets that can be used as collateral. Djibouti, Jordan, and Tajikistan launched geographically centralized, unified, and notice-based collateral registries in 2018/19. Moreover, Jordan, Kenya, and Tajikistan introduced online features to their existing registries. Twenty-three economies implemented reforms improving credit information systems. One of the most common features of reform was the expansion of coverage of individuals and firms in credit registries or bureaus. Six developing countries carried out this type of reform. Niger, Senegal, and Togo, for example, passed laws allowing the credit bureau, Creditinfo VoLo, to collect broader historical data. With more credit data and data from alternative sources, these three economies were able to boost coverage rates.

For the ninth year in a row, the most common feature of reforms in paying taxes is the implementation or enhancement of electronic filing and payment systems. Seventeen economies carried out such reforms in calendar year 2018. In terms of digitization, the most notable progress since *Doing Business 2006* has been achieved in Europe and Central Asia. Today taxes can be filed electronically in 22 economies in this region, compared to only 4 in 2004.

Economies across all regions reformed aspects of international trade logistics in 2018/19, with 25 making it easier to move goods across borders. More than 40% of the reforms captured by the trading across borders indicators were in low- and lower-middle-income economies. Overall, South Asia was the region with the highest share of economies implementing trade reforms in *Doing Business 2020*. Trade reforms demonstrate the importance of cross-border cooperation in ensuring easy customs clearance procedures, harmonization of compliance rules, and border control efficiency. Nepal, for example, decreased the time to export and import by opening a new joint border crossing point with India.

In the area of contract enforcement, eight economies provided more straightforward options—outside of ordinary courts or procedures—for resolving legal disputes. Mauritania and Moldova, for example, implemented fast-track procedures as an effective way to resolve small-value disputes. Three economies in Latin America and the Caribbean adopted techniques intended to ensure a timely and organized flow of cases through the court system. Jamaica started publishing court performance reports, Costa Rica introduced a pretrial conference, and Paraguay implemented an electronic case management system.

Thirteen economies implemented reforms making it easier to resolve insolvency. A characteristic feature of these reforms was the introduction of a reorganization procedure. Keeping viable businesses afloat is one of the most important objectives of bankruptcy systems. The highest recovery rates are recorded in economies where reorganization is the most common insolvency proceeding for viable businesses in financial distress. Bahrain, Jordan, and Saudi Arabia all introduced reorganization proceedings, completely overhauling their previous insolvency frameworks.

Eleven economies made changes to employment regulations. The OECD high-income group recorded the highest share of reforms, with work scheduling being the most common feature. Austria increased overtime to 60 hours per week, and Hungary raised its overtime allowance to 400 hours per calendar year, making employment regulation more business-friendly. Conversely, the Slovak Republic increased wage premiums for work on weekly rest days and at night. North Macedonia reduced the length of the probationary period (to four months from six), introduced priority rules in the case of both redundancy dismissals and reemployment, and increased severance payments.

When doing business is not easy

Not all regulatory changes make it easier for entrepreneurs to do business. In 2018/19, 26 economies introduced 31 reforms that stifled efficiency. Some changes are a conscious trade-off. Croatia's credit bureau, for example, stopped distributing data on individuals while it gauges the full extent of the European Union General Data Protection Regulation. In the area of protecting minority investors, Belarus extended the deadline for companies to inform the market of related-party transactions. This change makes it easier for firms to comply with regulation but increases information asymmetry, which could be harmful to investors. Political changes also play a role. In Sudan, the new majority in the National Assembly did not endorse temporary amendments to the Companies Act. As a result, a lapse in the provisions adversely affected Sudan's performance on the indicators for getting credit, protecting minority investors, and resolving insolvency.

Increased regulatory costs faced by the private sector serve as another foundation for changes making it more difficult to do business, as evident in 16 of the 31 cases. Increasing the cost to do business can be counterproductive. Studies show that higher business start-up costs adversely affect the number of new market entrants.[9] Firms that never incorporate because of prohibitive expenses represent a compounding net loss of public revenue. In other cases, the administrative costs associated with enacting comparatively minor fee increases may not even be covered by slightly increased revenues. For example, Cambodia increased costs associated with registration with the Ministry of Labor and Vocational Training. Mexico (Mexico City) increased the fees for obtaining a building permit. The Bahamas increased the stamp duty for property transfers while Nepal hiked up the registration fee to transfer properties.

Insufficient reform follow-through, as in several economies, is another reason for a deterioration in the business climate. Morocco, for instance, stopped publishing statistics on the number of property transactions and land disputes. And Belarus weakened minority investor protections by no longer requiring immediate public disclosure of related-party transactions. Some reforms are relatively easy to initiate; however, without proper upkeep, their benefits can fail to materialize.

Finally, design and implementation issues undermine reform efforts. Changing the agency in charge of property registration in Kazakhstan had the potential to improve service delivery. Because the new entity was not authorized to collect state duties, however, users had to make some payments at a different location. Mali made paying taxes more difficult by introducing a new tax—the solidarity contribution—which is an additional cost on businesses imposed on turnover. Barbados rendered property transfers less efficient by increasing the time to record the conveyance at the Land Registry as well as pay transfer fees and stamp duties.

What is new in this year's study?

Doing Business 2020 features three case studies—on business regulatory reforms across four indicator sets (starting a business, getting credit, paying taxes, and resolving insolvency), on contracting with the government, and on employing workers. The case study on reforms analyzes prominent regulatory changes implemented by governments since the inception of *Doing Business*. Among the most common regulatory changes over the past 17 years are simplifying the requirements to start a company, easing tax compliance burdens, increasing access to credit, and ensuring the survival of viable businesses. The case study also discusses the effects of regulatory changes on various dimensions of economic development and investment activity.

The contracting with the government case study measures the efficiency of public procurement. The case study describes a standardized scenario benchmarked by the indicator set and outlines a preliminary description of the methodology. Worldwide, public procurement accounts for 10–25% of GDP on average, and cumulatively governments spend $10 trillion on public contracts every year. The efficiency of the process varies considerably, however; currently, there are no global data to benchmark such practices. The contracting with the government database constitutes a repository of comparable data on how procurement processes are carried out. This indicator set, which has been under development for the past three years, will be included in the ease of doing business score in *Doing Business 2021*.

The case study on employing workers highlights the positive effects of flexible employment regulation for firms, which in turn affects job creation and productivity growth. It analyzes the advantages of operating under a less rigid hiring framework that, for example, permits fixed-term contracts. In light of the changing dynamics of work, the case study further examines the benefits of flexible rules on working hours. It shows that restrictions on dismissal due to redundancy hurt firms as well as youth employment. *Doing Business 2020* also includes a literature review chapter on relevant research articles published in top-ranking economic journals since 2013.

Notes

1. Djankov 2016.
2. Heckelman 2000.
3. Herrendorf and Teixeira 2011.
4. The figure excludes seven economies with a minimum capital requirement of less than $5.
5. Transparency International database. A higher score on the Corruption Perceptions Index indicates a lower level of perceived corruption.
6. Economies are selected on the basis of the number of reforms and ranked on how much their ease of doing business score improved. First, *Doing Business* selects the economies that implemented reforms making it easier to do business in 3 or more of the 10 areas included in this year's aggregate ease of doing business score. Regulatory changes making it more difficult to do business are subtracted from the number of those making it easier. Second, *Doing Business* ranks these economies on the increase in their ease of doing business score due to reforms from the previous year (the impact due to changes in income per capita and the lending rate is excluded). The improvement in their score is calculated not by using the data published in 2018 but by using comparable data that capture data revisions and methodology changes when applicable. The choice of the most improved economies is determined by the largest improvements in the ease of doing business score among those with at least three reforms. The order of economies is based on the difference of unrounded scores.
7. Considering the areas that constitute the ease of doing business ranking.
8. Ramalho and Saltane 2019.
9. Djankov and others 2002; Klapper, Laeven, and Rajan 2006.

CHAPTER 1

About *Doing Business*

- *Doing Business* measures aspects of business regulation affecting small domestic firms located in the largest business city of 190 economies. In addition, for 11 economies a second city is covered.
- *Doing Business* covers 12 areas of business regulation. Ten of these areas—starting a business, dealing with construction permits, getting electricity, registering property, getting credit, protecting minority investors, paying taxes, trading across borders, enforcing contracts, and resolving insolvency—are included in the ease of doing business score and ease of doing business ranking. *Doing Business* also measures regulation on employing workers and contracting with the government, which are not included in the ease of doing business score and ranking.
- More than 48,000 professionals in 190 economies have assisted in providing the data that inform the *Doing Business* indicators.

Doing Business is founded on the principle that economic activity benefits from clear rules: rules that allow voluntary exchanges between economic actors, set out strong property rights, facilitate the resolution of commercial disputes, and provide contractual partners with protections against arbitrariness and abuse. Such rules are much more effective in promoting growth and development when they are efficient, transparent, and accessible to those for whom they are intended.

Rules create an environment where new entrants with drive and innovative ideas can get started in business and where productive firms can invest, expand, and create new jobs. The role of government policy in the daily operations of small and medium-size domestic firms is a central focus of the *Doing Business* data. The objective is to encourage regulation that is efficient, transparent, and easy to implement so that businesses can thrive. *Doing Business* data focus on 12 areas of regulation affecting small and medium-size domestic firms in the largest business city of an economy. The project uses standardized case studies to provide objective, quantitative measures that can be compared across 190 economies.

What *Doing Business* measures

Doing Business captures several important dimensions of the regulatory environment affecting domestic firms. It provides quantitative indicators on regulation for starting a business, dealing with construction permits, getting electricity, registering property, getting credit, protecting minority investors, paying taxes, trading across borders, enforcing contracts, and resolving insolvency (table 1.1). *Doing Business* also measures aspects of employing workers and contracting with the government (public procurement), which are not included in the ranking.

How the indicators are selected

The design of the *Doing Business* indicators has been informed by theoretical insights gleaned from extensive research.[1] In addition, background papers developing the methodology for most of the *Doing Business* indicator sets have established the importance of the rules and regulations that *Doing Business* measures for economic outcomes such as trade volumes, foreign direct investment, market capitalization in stock exchanges, and private credit as a percentage of GDP.[2]

Some *Doing Business* indicators give a higher score for more regulation and better-functioning institutions (such as courts or credit bureaus). Higher scores are given for stricter disclosure requirements for related-party transactions, for example, in the area of protecting minority investors. Higher scores are also given for a simplified way of applying regulation that keeps compliance costs for firms low—such as by easing the burden of business start-up formalities with a one-stop shop or through a single online portal. Finally, the scores reward economies that apply a risk-based approach to regulation as a way to address social and environmental concerns—such

TABLE 1.1 What *Doing Business* measures—12 areas of business regulation

Indicator set	What is measured
Starting a business	Procedures, time, cost, and paid-in minimum capital to start a limited liability company for men and women
Dealing with construction permits	Procedures, time, and cost to complete all formalities to build a warehouse and the quality control and safety mechanisms in the construction permitting system
Getting electricity	Procedures, time, and cost to get connected to the electrical grid; the reliability of the electricity supply; and the transparency of tariffs
Registering property	Procedures, time, and cost to transfer a property and the quality of the land administration system for men and women
Getting credit	Movable collateral laws and credit information systems
Protecting minority investors	Minority shareholders' rights in related-party transactions and in corporate governance
Paying taxes	Payments, time, and total tax and contribution rate for a firm to comply with all tax regulations as well as postfiling processes
Trading across borders	Time and cost to export the product of comparative advantage and to import auto parts
Enforcing contracts	Time and cost to resolve a commercial dispute and the quality of judicial processes for men and women
Resolving insolvency	Time, cost, outcome, and recovery rate for a commercial insolvency and the strength of the legal framework for insolvency
Employing workers	Flexibility in employment regulation
Contracting with the government	Procedures and time to participate in and win a works contract through public procurement and the public procurement regulatory framework

Note: The employing workers and contracting with the government indicator sets are not part of the ease of doing business ranking in *Doing Business 2020.*

as by placing a greater regulatory burden on activities that pose a high risk to the population and a lesser one on lower-risk activities. Thus, the economies that rank highest on the ease of doing business are not those where there is no regulation, but those where governments have managed to create rules that facilitate interactions in the marketplace without needlessly hindering the development of the private sector.

Doing Business 2020 does not introduce any new metrics. The assumptions of the protecting minority investors indicator set, however, refocused on corporate governance for listed companies so that, if an economy does not have an active stock exchange with at least 10 listings that are not state-owned, no points are given under the extent of shareholder governance index. Economies are assessed on the same practices as before.

The ease of doing business score and ease of doing business ranking

To provide different perspectives on the data, *Doing Business* presents data both for individual indicators and for two aggregate measures: the ease of doing business score and the ease of doing business ranking. The ease of doing business score aids in assessing the absolute level of regulatory performance and how it improves over time. The individual indicator scores show the distance of each economy from the best regulatory performance observed in each of the indicators across all economies in the *Doing Business* sample since 2005 or the third year in which data were collected for the indicator. The best regulatory performance is set at the highest possible value for indicators calculated as scores, such as the strength of legal rights index or the quality of land administration index. This approach underscores the gap between a particular economy's performance and the best regulatory performance at any time and is used to assess the absolute change in the economy's regulatory environment over time as measured by *Doing Business* (see chapter 7 on the ease of doing business score and ease of doing business ranking). The ranking on the ease of doing business complements the ease of doing business score by providing information about an economy's performance in business regulation relative to the performance of other economies as measured by *Doing Business*.

Doing Business uses a simple averaging approach for weighting component indicators, calculating rankings, and determining the ease of doing business score.[3] Each topic covered by *Doing Business* relates to a different aspect of the business regulatory environment. The scores and rankings of each economy vary considerably across topics, indicating that a strong performance by an economy in one area of regulation can coexist with weak performance in another (figure 1.1). One way to assess the variability of an economy's regulatory performance is to look at its scores across topics. Panama, for example, has an overall ease of doing business score of 66.6, meaning that it is about two-thirds of the way up the range from the worst to the best performance. It scores highly at 92.0 on starting a business,

FIGURE 1.1 An economy's regulatory environment may be more business-friendly in some areas than in others

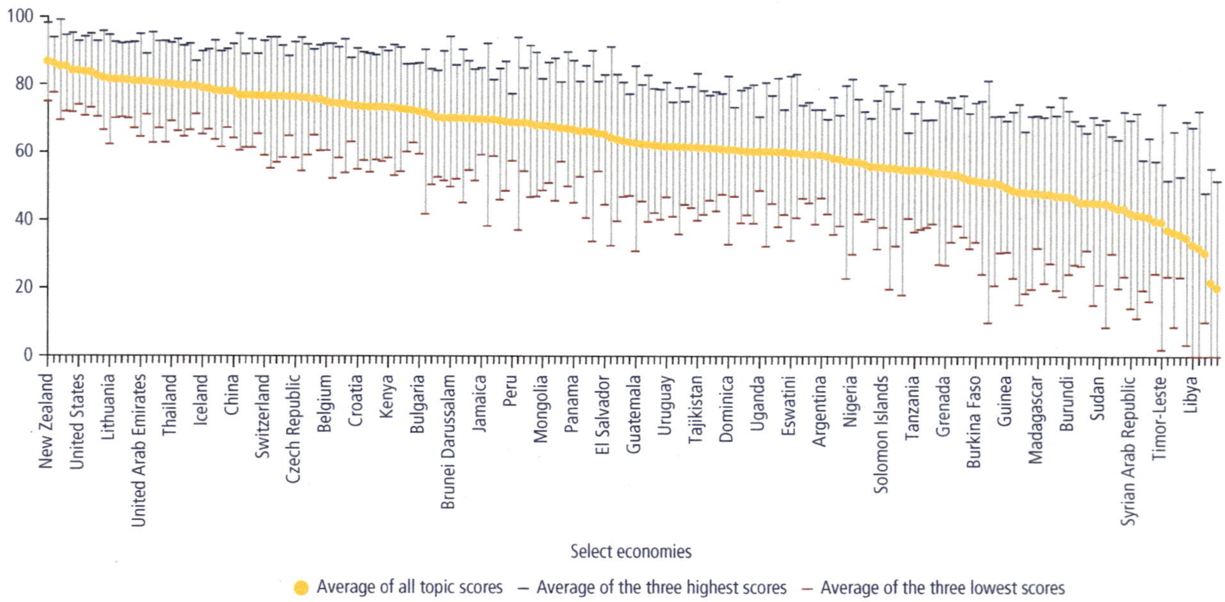

Source: Doing Business database.

Note: The scores reflected are those for the 10 *Doing Business* topics included in this year's aggregate ease of doing business score. The figure is illustrative only; it does not include all 190 economies covered by *Doing Business 2020*. See the *Doing Business* website for the scores for each *Doing Business* topic for all economies.

85.5 on trading across borders, and 83.5 on getting electricity. At the same time, it has a score of 49.0 for enforcing contracts, 46.7 for paying taxes, and 39.5 for resolving insolvency.

Advantages and limitations of the methodology

The *Doing Business* methodology is designed to be an easily replicable way to benchmark specific characteristics of business regulation—how they are implemented by governments and experienced by private firms on the ground. Its advantages and limitations should be understood when using the data.

Ensuring comparability of the data across a global set of economies is a central consideration for the *Doing Business* indicators, which are developed using standardized case scenarios with specific assumptions. One such assumption is the location of a standardized business—the subject of the *Doing Business* case study—in the largest business city of the economy. The reality is that business regulations and their enforcement may differ within a country, particularly in federal states and large economies. Gathering data for every relevant jurisdiction in each of the 190 economies covered by *Doing Business* is infeasible. Nevertheless, where policy makers are interested in generating data at the local level, beyond the largest business city, and learning from local good practices, *Doing Business* has complemented its global indicators with subnational studies. Also, starting with *Doing Business 2015*, coverage was extended to the second-largest city in economies with a population of more than 100 million (as of 2013).

Doing Business recognizes the limitations of the standardized case scenarios and assumptions. Although such assumptions come at the expense of generality, they also ensure the comparability of data. Some *Doing Business* topics are complex, so it is important that the standardized cases are defined carefully. For example, the standardized case scenario usually involves a limited liability company or its legal equivalent. There are two reasons for this assumption. First, private limited liability companies are the most prevalent business form (for firms with more than one owner) in many economies around the world. Second, this choice reflects the focus of *Doing Business* on expanding opportunities for entrepreneurship: investors are encouraged to venture into business when potential losses are limited to their capital participation.

Another assumption underlying the *Doing Business* indicators is that entrepreneurs have knowledge of and comply with applicable regulations. In practice, entrepreneurs may not be aware of what needs to be done or how to comply with regulations and may lose considerable time trying to find out. Alternatively, they may intentionally avoid compliance—by not registering for social security, for example. Firms may opt for bribery and other informal arrangements intended to bypass the rules where regulation is particularly onerous. Levels of informality tend to be higher in economies with especially burdensome regulation. Compared with their formal sector counterparts, firms in the informal sector typically grow more slowly, have poorer access to credit, and employ fewer workers—and these workers remain outside the protections of labor law and, more generally, other legal protections embedded in the law.[4] Firms in the informal sector are also less likely to pay taxes. *Doing Business* measures one set of factors that help explain the occurrence of informality, and it provides policy makers with insights into potential areas of regulatory reform.

Many important policy areas are not covered by *Doing Business*; even within the areas it measures, the scope is narrow. *Doing Business* does not measure the full range of factors, policies, and institutions that affect the quality of an economy's business environment or its national competitiveness. It does not, for example, capture aspects of macroeconomic stability, development of the financial system, market size, the incidence of bribery and corruption, or the quality of the labor force.

Data collection in practice

The *Doing Business* data are based on a detailed reading of domestic laws, regulations, and administrative requirements as well as their implementation in practice as experienced by private professionals. The study covers 190 economies—including some of the smallest and poorest economies, for which other sources provide little or no data. The data are collected through several rounds of communication with expert respondents (both private sector practitioners and government officials), through responses to questionnaires, conference calls, written correspondence, and visits by the team. *Doing Business* relies on four main sources of information: the relevant laws and regulations, *Doing Business* respondents, the governments of the economies covered, and the World Bank Group regional staff (figure 1.2). For a detailed explanation of the *Doing Business* methodology, see the data notes at www.doingbusiness.org.

Relevant laws and regulations

The *Doing Business* indicators are based mostly on laws and regulations: approximately two-thirds of the data embedded in the *Doing Business* indicators are based on a reading of the law. In addition to filling out questionnaires, *Doing Business* respondents submit references to the relevant laws, regulations, and fee schedules. The *Doing Business* team collects the texts of the relevant laws and regulations and checks the questionnaire responses for accuracy. The team examines the civil procedure code, for example, to check the maximum number of adjournments in a commercial court dispute, and reads the insolvency code to identify if the debtor can initiate liquidation or reorganization proceedings. Because the data collection process involves an annual update of an established database, having a very large sample of respondents is not strictly necessary. In principle,

FIGURE 1.2 How *Doing Business* collects and verifies the data

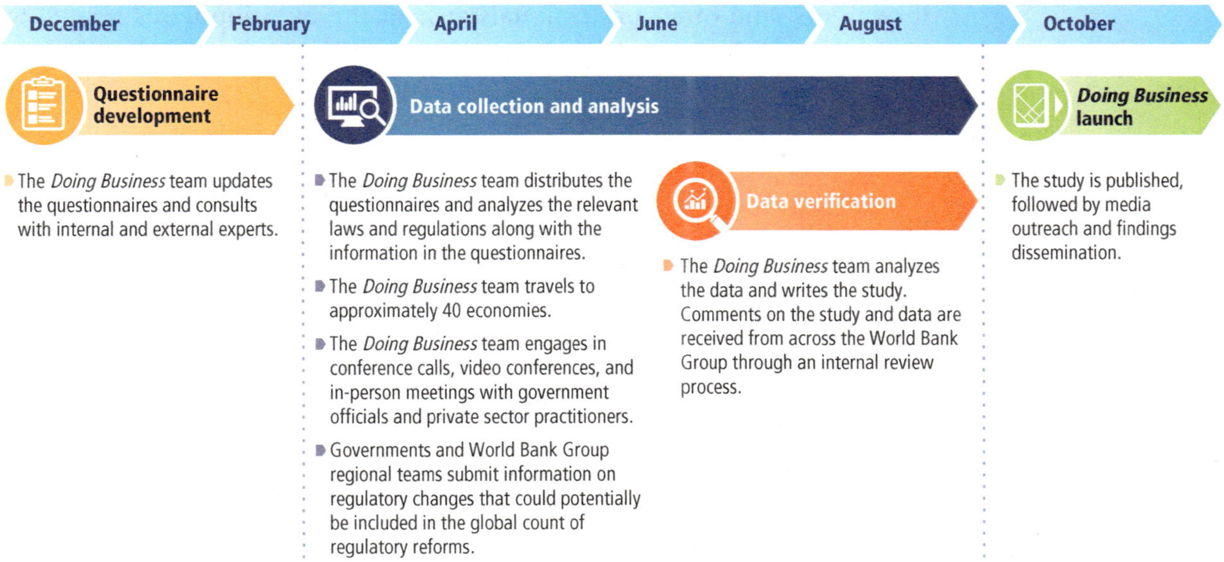

the role of the contributors is largely advisory—helping the *Doing Business* team to locate and understand the laws and regulations. There are quickly diminishing returns to an expanded pool of contributors. This notwithstanding, the number of contributors rose by 80% between 2010 and 2019.

Extensive consultations with multiple contributors are conducted by the team to minimize measurement errors for the rest of the data. For some indicators—for example, those on dealing with construction permits, enforcing contracts, and resolving insolvency—the time component and part of the cost component (where fee schedules are lacking) are based on actual practice rather than the law on the books. This approach introduces a degree of judgment by respondents on what actual practice looks like. When respondents disagree, the time indicators reported by *Doing Business* represent the median values of several responses given under the assumptions of the standardized case.

Doing Business respondents

More than 48,000 professionals in 190 economies have assisted in providing the data that inform the *Doing Business* indicators over the past 17 years.[5] *Doing Business 2020* draws on the inputs of more than 15,000 professionals.[6] The *Doing Business* website shows the number of respondents for each economy and each indicator set.

Selected on the basis of their expertise in these areas, respondents are professionals who routinely administer or advise on the legal and regulatory requirements in the specific areas covered by *Doing Business*. Because of the focus on legal and regulatory arrangements, most of the respondents are legal professionals such as lawyers, judges, or notaries.

In addition, officials of the credit bureau or registry complete the credit information questionnaire. Accountants, architects, engineers, freight forwarders, and other professionals answer the questionnaires related to paying taxes, dealing with construction permits, trading across borders, and getting electricity. Certain public officials (such as registrars from the company or property registry) also provide information that is incorporated into the indicators.

The *Doing Business* approach is to work with legal practitioners or other professionals who regularly undertake the transactions involved. Following the standard methodological approach for time-and-motion studies, *Doing Business* breaks down each process or transaction, such as starting a business or registering a property into separate steps to ensure a better estimate of time. The time estimate for each step is given by practitioners who have significant and routine experience in the transaction.

Governments and World Bank Group regional staff

After receiving the completed questionnaires from the *Doing Business* respondents, verifying the information against the law, and conducting follow-up inquiries to ensure that all relevant information is captured, the *Doing Business* team sends the regulatory reform descriptions to the World Bank Group's Board of Executive Directors and World Bank Group Country Management Units in different regions, which then inform the respective governments about the reforms identified in their economies. Through this process, government authorities and World Bank Group staff working on the economies covered by *Doing Business* can alert the *Doing Business* team about, for example, regulatory reforms not reported by the respondents or additional achievements of regulatory reforms. In addition, the team responds formally to the comments of governments or regional staff and provides explanations of the scoring decisions.

Data adjustments

Information on data corrections is provided in the data notes available at the *Doing Business* website. A transparent complaint procedure allows anyone to challenge the data. From November 2018 to October 2019, the team received and responded to 150 queries on the data.

Uses of the *Doing Business* data

Doing Business was designed with two main types of users in mind: policy makers and researchers. It is a tool that governments can use to design sound business regulatory policies. Nevertheless, the *Doing Business* data are limited in scope and should be complemented with other sources of information. *Doing Business* focuses on a few specific rules relevant to the case studies analyzed. These rules and case studies are chosen to be illustrative of the business regulatory environment, but they do not constitute a comprehensive description of that environment. By providing a unique dataset that enables analysis aimed at better understanding the role of business regulation in economic development, *Doing Business* is also an important source of information for researchers.

Governments and policy makers

Doing Business offers policy makers a benchmarking tool useful in stimulating policy debate, both by exposing potential challenges and by identifying good practices and lessons learned. Despite the narrow focus of the indicators, the initial debate in an economy on the results they highlight typically turns into a deeper discussion on areas where business regulatory reform is needed, including areas well beyond those measured by *Doing Business*. In economies where subnational studies are conducted, the *Doing Business* indicators go one step further in offering policy makers a tool to identify good practices that can be adopted within their economies.

The *Doing Business* indicators are "actionable." For example, governments set the minimum capital requirement for new firms, invest in company and property registries to increase their efficiency, or improve the efficiency of tax administration by adopting the latest technology to facilitate the preparation, filing, and payment of taxes by the business community. Governments also undertake court reforms to shorten delays in the enforcement of contracts. Some *Doing Business* indicators, however, capture procedures, time, and costs that involve private sector participants, such as lawyers, notaries, architects, electricians, or freight forwarders. Governments have little influence in the short run over the fees these professions charge, though much can be achieved by strengthening professional licensing regimes and preventing anticompetitive behavior. In addition, governments have no control over the geographic location of their economy, a factor that can adversely affect businesses.

Over the past decade governments have increasingly turned to *Doing Business* as a repository of actionable, objective data providing unique insights into good practices worldwide as they have come to understand the importance of business regulation as a driving force of competitiveness. To ensure the coordination of efforts across agencies, economies such as Colombia, Kuwait, and Malaysia have formed regulatory reform committees. These committees use the *Doing Business* indicators as one input to inform their programs for improving the business environment. More than 70 other economies have also formed such committees. Governments have reported more than 3,800 regulatory reforms, 1,316 of which have been informed by *Doing Business* since 2003.[7]

Many economies share knowledge on the regulatory reform process related to the areas measured by *Doing Business*. Among the most common venues for this knowledge sharing are peer-to-peer learning events—workshops where officials from different governments across a region or even across the globe meet to discuss the challenges of regulatory reform and to share their experiences.

Researchers

Doing Business data are widely used by researchers in academia, think tanks, international organizations, and other institutions. Since 2003, thousands of empirical articles have used *Doing Business* data or its conceptual framework to analyze the impact of business regulation on various economic outcomes.[8] *Doing Business 2020* presents a literature review of recent research on the effects of business regulation in chapter 2. That chapter is an update to a similar exercise conducted in *Doing Business 2014* and focuses on research published in the top 100 academic journals in economics between 2013 and 2019.[9]

What is next?

Doing Business 2021 will include the contracting with the government indicator set in the calculation of the ease of doing business ranking. The contracting with the government indicator set measures the procedures and time to win a public procurement contract according to a standardized case study focused on the infrastructure sector (see chapter 5 on contracting with the government). It also assesses the compliance of regulation with internationally recognized good practice. The data benchmark the efficiency of the public procurement life cycle in the 190 economies measured by *Doing Business*. As in the case of the other topics included in *Doing Business*, the data identify sources of delay and waste of resources.

Also, as part of a five-year cycle established in *Doing Business 2015*, *Doing Business 2021* will update the metrics of the best and worst regulatory performance used in the calculation of the scores for the various *Doing Business* indicator sets as well as the data on gross national income per capita and the export and import products used as a reference for each economy in the trading across borders indicator set. This update will allow the *Doing Business* data to more accurately reflect the best regulatory practices achieved by top-performing economies in the last five years—these practices will set the new standard for other economies to pursue. *Doing Business* is also considering expanding the coverage of the study to include the second-largest business city for economies with a population of more than 100 million (as of 2019), and the third- and fourth-largest business cities for economies with a population of more than 300 million.

Notes

1. Djankov 2016.
2. These papers are available on the *Doing Business* website at http://www.doingbusiness.org/methodology.
3. For getting credit, indicators are weighted proportionally, according to their contribution to the total score, with a weight of 60% assigned to the strength of legal rights index and 40% to the depth of credit information index. In this way, each point included in these indexes has the same value independent of the component it belongs to. Indicators for all other topics are assigned equal weights. For more details, see chapter 7 on the ease of doing business score and ease of doing business ranking.

4. La Porta and Shleifer 2008; Schneider 2005.
5. The annual data collection exercise is an update of the database. The *Doing Business* team and the contributors examine the extent to which the regulatory framework has changed in ways relevant for the features captured by the indicators. The data collection process should therefore be seen as adding each year to an existing stock of knowledge reflected in the previous year's edition, not as creating an entirely new dataset.
6. Although about 15,000 contributors provided data for *Doing Business 2020*, many of them completed a questionnaire for more than one *Doing Business* indicator set. Indeed, the total number of contributions received for *Doing Business 2020* is more than 18,400, which represents a true measure of the inputs received. The average number of contributions per indicator set and economy is more than seven. For more details, see http://www.doingbusiness.org/contributors/doing-business.
7. These are reforms for which *Doing Business* is aware that information provided by *Doing Business* was used in shaping the reform agenda.
8. Since the publication of the first *Doing Business* study in 2003, more than 3,700 research articles discussing how regulation in the areas measured by *Doing Business* influences economic outcomes have been published in peer-reviewed academic journals; over 1,300 of these are published in the top 100 journals. Another 10,000 are published as working papers, books, reports, dissertations, or research notes.
9. The journal and institution rankings are from Research Papers in Economics (RePEc) and cover the last 10 years. They can be accessed at https://ideas.repec.org/top/top.journals.simple10.html and https://ideas.repec.org/top/top.inst.allbest10.html.

CHAPTER 2

The effects of business regulation

- Since 2003, nearly 4,000 articles using *Doing Business* data have been published in peer-reviewed academic journals and more than 10,000 working papers have been posted online.
- Improvements in firm entry regulation are associated with higher productivity.
- Better land property rights improve investment decisions by individuals.
- Court efficiency plays a major role in the process of economic development.

Doing Business provides annual cross-country data on how governments regulate business, enabling research on how regulation affects development. Thousands of empirical studies have assessed how the regulatory environment for business affects productivity, growth, employment, trade, investment, access to finance, and the size of the informal economy. Since 2003, when *Doing Business* was first published, numerous articles discussing how regulation in the areas measured by the study influences economic outcomes have been published in peer-reviewed academic journals. Over 10,000 additional working papers have been posted online.[1]

Doing Business 2014 reviewed research articles—including those published in top-ranking economics journals between 2008 and 2013 or disseminated as working papers in 2012/13—that used *Doing Business* data for analysis or motivation.[2] This chapter updates that review, adding research articles published between January 2013 and July 2019.

Firm entry

Changes to start-up regulation affect the number and size of firms in the market. New firm entry results in higher productivity through the reallocation of resources from old to new firms. Fernandes, Ferreira, and Winters (2018) find that the entry-simplifying reform introduced in Portugal in 2005 boosted sectoral competition. Using employer–employee data for all private sector firms and workers in the country, they also find that higher competition is associated with better firm performance. Furthermore, greater market competition is associated with an increase of 6–11% in executive remuneration. Alfaro and Chari (2014) examine the effects of the "License Raj" reform in India on firm size distribution and resource reallocation. The authors find that the number of small firms increased in industries with easier start-up rules. They also observe an increase in the productivity of these sectors, suggesting a reduction in resource allocation distortions over the same period.

Meeting start-up requirements involves additional costs for firms. An implicit assumption is that firms benefit from start-up registration in the form of expanded access to credit—legal protection compensates for the additional costs of becoming formal. Testing this hypothesis using data from Benin, Benhassine and others (2018) find that start-up registration did not improve the sales or profits of an average firm. Testing the benefits of eased start-up regulation in Vietnam, however, Demenet, Razafindrakoto, and Roubaud (2016) find that the value added of firms increased by 20% on average.

Property transfer

Private land rights facilitate greater access to credit. Using enterprise data, Karas, Pyle, and Schoors (2015) evaluate the effect of greater land tenure security among large urban industrial businesses in the Russian Federation and find that private land rights facilitate access to external financing and promote investment.

When property rights are not secure, fear of expropriation may drive entrepreneurs to make suboptimal investment decisions. Goldstein and others (2018) analyze the benefits of strengthening land property rights in rural Benin by examining the link between land demarcation and investment. The authors find that the land tenure security improvements of demarcation induce a 23–43% shift toward long-term investment on demarcated land parcels. They also find that improved tenure security leads households to shift their investment decisions from subsistence to perennial cash crops and that female-headed households are more responsive than male-headed households to the demarcation reform.

Reliability of electricity

Power outages represent a significant obstacle to doing business in economies worldwide. An unreliable supply of electricity results in spoiled perishable goods, damage to sensitive equipment, and productivity losses. Firms adapt by buying generators and other expensive equipment to protect sensitive inventory and machinery. Allcott, Collard-Wexler, and O'Connell (2016) examine the effects of electricity shortages on input choices, revenue, and productivity in manufacturing plants in India between 1992 and 2010. The authors find that electrical shortages reduce the average plant's revenue by 6–8%, and that producer surplus drops by 10%, of which roughly half is due to the cost of backup generators. Moyo (2013) investigates the relationship between power outages and manufacturing productivity in Africa in 2002–05 and finds a negative relationship between both the number of hours per day without electricity and the percentage of output lost due to outages and productivity.

Andersen and Dalgaard (2013) also focus on African businesses in estimating the impact of power outages on economic growth over the period 1995–2007. The authors find that a 1-percentage-point increase in outages decreases long-run GDP per capita by 3%. Using firm-level data for 14 Sub-Saharan African economies, Cole and others (2018) find that reducing average outage levels to those of South Africa would increase overall sales of firms by 85%, and the increase would rise to nearly 120% for firms without a generator (figure 2.1).

Labor market regulation

Changes in labor market regulation affect unemployment rates and labor force participation. Labor market regulation also determines firm productivity.

When set above the market equilibrium salary, minimum wages raise unemployment in competitive markets. Using data for 2001–09, Jales (2018) finds that the introduction of a minimum wage in Brazil is

FIGURE 2.1 Reducing power outages boosts overall firm performance

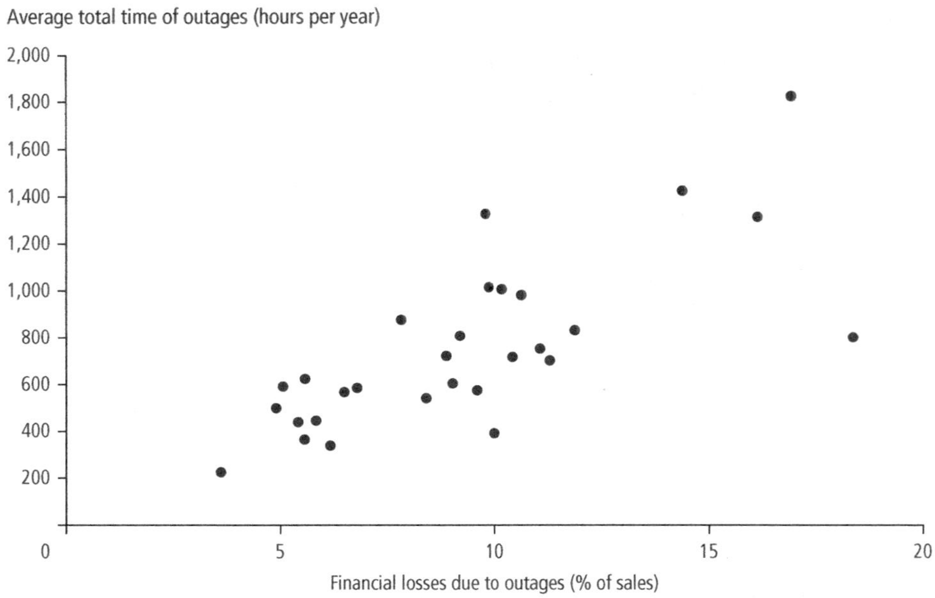

Source: Cole and others 2018.
Note: Financial losses are positively correlated with the average total time of outages.

associated with a 39% increase in informal employment. Yamada (2016) finds that the introduction of a minimum wage in Indonesia resulted in a reduction in both hours of work and employment. Although noting an increase in earnings among low- and middle-income households, the author concludes that the welfare gain resulting from raising the minimum wage is negligible.

Alvarez and Fuentes (2018) find that a minimum wage increase in Chile under rigid labor market regulation is partially responsible for a slowdown in manufacturing productivity in the late 1990s. The authors estimate that a real increase of about 22% in the minimum wage during the period 1998–2000 reduced total factor productivity by 2% in industries with fewer unskilled workers and 4% in those with more unskilled workers. Bjuggren (2018) finds that increased labor market flexibility in Sweden is associated with higher labor productivity. In particular, the author examines the effects of a 2001 reform of employment protection rules that allowed firms with fewer than 11 workers to exempt 2 workers from seniority rules (under which the last person hired is the first to be fired in the case of redundancy).

Amirapu and Gechter (2019) find that restrictive labor regulation in India is associated with a 35% increase in firms' unit labor costs. Kawaguchi and Murao (2014), using data from high-income economies from 1960 to 2010, find that the persistence of youth unemployment is positively correlated with labor market rigidity. A study by Acharya, Baghai, and Subramanian (2013) suggests, however, that limited labor market rigidity in some high-income economies is positively correlated with firm innovation, primarily because job stability boosts employee innovation.

Changes to labor market regulation are associated with changes in credit markets. Alimov (2015) analyzes the impact of employment protection regulation on bank lending in 25 high-income economies and finds that increases in employment protection lead to greater loan spreads. He also finds that increases in employment protection result in bank loans that are significantly smaller and have shorter maturities.

Trade regulation and costs

The *Doing Business* indicators on trading across borders measure the time to clear official procedures, including customs controls. A growing body of literature uses these data. Martincus, Carballo, and Graziano (2015) measure the effects of customs-related delays on firms' exports by studying export transactions data from Uruguay for the period 2002–11, including the actual time it took for these transactions to clear customs. Their findings suggest that a 10% increase in customs delays results in a 4% decline in exports. This effect emanates from higher costs for exporters, which subsequently reduce their foreign sales, as well as for buyers, which appear to reduce their exposure to firms whose deliveries are subject to such delays. Similarly, Hornok and Koren (2015) analyze the impact of administrative per-shipment costs on trade volumes. Employing Spanish shipment-level export data for the period 2006–12, the authors find that a 50% reduction in per-shipment costs is equivalent to a 9-percentage-point reduction in tariffs.

Court efficiency

Judicial reforms targeting the quality, speed, and access of the judiciary favor improvements in productivity and economic development. Chemin (2018) finds that these reforms improved firm productivity by 22% in sectors requiring more relationship-specific investments.

Judicial efficiency is essential to firm productivity. Ahsan (2013) uses firm-level data from India to study the complementarities between the speed of contract enforcement and tariff liberalization. His findings suggest that the gains in productivity from a reduction in input tariffs are highest for firms in economies with the most efficient courts.

Gianfreda and Vallanti (2017) analyze the impact of court delays in settling labor disputes in Italy. The authors argue that delays in trials of labor disputes increase firing costs. They also show that the rate of job turnover is significantly lower in judicial districts with longer trials.[3]

Efficient courts improve financial markets. Ponticelli and Alencar (2016) find that firms operating in Brazilian municipalities with less congested civil courts experienced a larger increase in the use of secured loans. In the years following a reform that increased the protection of secured creditors, firms also experienced a significant increase in investment and output value. These results underscore the importance of the timely enforcement of creditors' rights by the courts to improve access to finance.[4]

Faster and cheaper access to justice reduces some of the obstacles faced by entrepreneurs. Lichand and Soares (2014) analyze the creation of special civil tribunals in São Paulo in the 1990s that expanded the geographic presence of the justice system, simplified judicial procedures, and increased the speed of dispute adjudication. They find that the implementation of the tribunals led to higher rates of entrepreneurship among individuals with higher levels of education.

Better access to long-term debt reduces the volatility of firm growth. Demirgüç-Kunt, Horváth, and Huizinga (2017) examine this link using firm-level data for 47 developing economies over the period 1995–2013. They find that better credit information systems and contract enforcement mechanisms supporting credit markets improve firm access to long-term finance.

Bankruptcy costs play a major role, during both crises and recoveries. Ordoñez (2013) argues that lending rates, investment, and output (measured by real GDP per capita) fall quickly during a crisis, but slowly during a recovery. This asymmetry is stronger in economies with greater bankruptcy costs (measured by the cost of bankruptcy, bankruptcy duration, and the recovery rate).

Chakraborty (2016) argues that higher-quality institutions help firms to invest in institutional-dependent inputs, which might affect a firm's performance. The author finds that, in India, judicial quality is a significant determinant of higher firm performance, for both exports and domestic sales. A conservative estimate suggests that a 10% increase in judicial quality increases firm sales by 1–2%.

Creditors' rights

Calomiris and others (2017) study the link between creditors' rights and credit from banks using microlevel data for 12 emerging market economies (figure 2.2). The authors posit that legal systems for movable collateral are usually weak—they limit the scope of the movable assets that can be used as collateral, lack centralized registries, and require court orders to enforce defaults. When the protection of creditors' rights for movable collateral improves, however, banks lend one-third more using the same level of collateral. The authors test which of the components (creation, monitoring, or enforcement) matter more and find that the monitoring and enforcement components are the most relevant, implying that the results are driven by the existence of collateral registries and the possibility of out-of-court enforcement, and not by the mere existence of laws.

FIGURE 2.2 Better protection of creditors' rights over movable assets is associated with a greater supply of movable-collateralized loans, relative to immovable assets

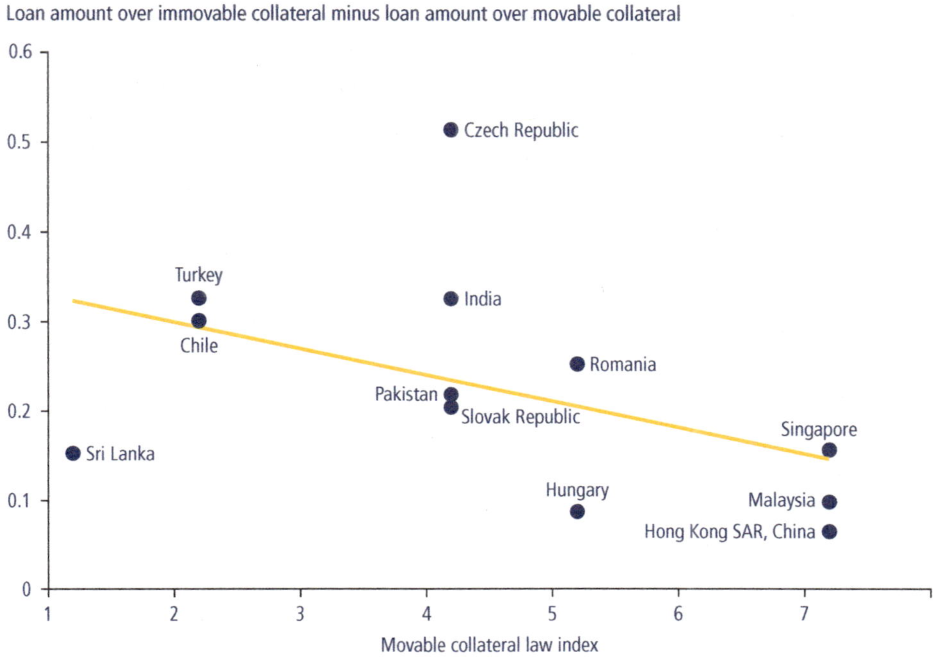

Source: Calomiris and others 2017.
Note: The movable collateral law index is based on seven of the eight components of the *Doing Business* strength of legal rights index published until 2013. The vertical axis measures the difference between the average loan-to-value of GlobalBank's loans backed by immovable assets and movable assets (machinery, inventory, and accounts receivable). Average for the period 2002–04.

Better protection of creditors' rights benefits firms, as long as the protections improve the efficiency of credit markets and access to funding. Berkowitz, Lin, and Ma (2015) study the complementarity between creditors' rights and firms' protections against the potential expropriation of their assets. Using data from China, the authors find that a reform reducing expropriation risks and improving creditors' rights led to an increase in firm value. By analyzing a securitization reform in India, however, Vig (2013) finds that the strengthening of creditors' rights introduces distortions that require firms to alter their debt structures by increasing liquidity.

Credit information

Credit information systems are intended to reduce the challenges of asymmetric information between borrowers and lenders. With the right infrastructure and regulation, credit bureaus allow lenders to identify the risks associated with borrowers. Doblas-Madrid and Minetti (2013) find that information sharing reduces contract delinquencies and defaults.

Specifically, lenders joining the bureau experience a drop of 23–30 days in the maximum number of days a borrower's payment is late (and a reduction of 6 days in the average number of days a payment is late). Furthermore, lenders joining the bureau were between 7% and 9% less likely on average to experience a serious delinquency (90 days or more past due); an even larger decline was observed in the probability of a major default event (such as debt collection or legal action). Dierkes and others (2013) find that business credit information sharing improves the quality of default predictions for German firms, especially for older firms and those with limited liability.

Firms identified as low risk by credit information systems enjoy better access to credit. For example, using firm-level data and credit scores for Belgian manufacturing firms between 1999 and 2007, Muûls (2015) finds that firms export and import more when they have better credit ratings and face lower credit constraints. The author argues that a firm's negative financial situation might make its overseas suppliers reluctant to trade with the firm, thereby affecting its imports. Being credit-constrained also prevents firms from overcoming the fixed costs associated with exporting and importing.

Other economic agents benefit indirectly from credit bureau signals. Beck, Lin, and Ma (2014) study the link between tax evasion and financial sector outreach using data for more than 64,000 firms across 102 economies for the period 2002–10. The authors show that firms evade taxes to a lesser degree in economies with better credit information sharing systems. This effect is stronger for smaller firms, firms in smaller cities and towns, as well as those operating in industries that rely on external financing, and in industries and economies with greater growth potential.

Shareholders' rights

Strong shareholders' rights are critical for the efficient operation of stock markets. Claessens, Ueda, and Yafeh (2014) study the relationship of those rights with the cost of capital using data from 40 economies for the period 1990–2007. The authors find that well-defined and well-enforced shareholders' rights reduce the overall cost of capital, especially for expanding or distressed firms. They also find that the extent of creditors' rights does not have significant effects on the cost of capital. Houston, Lin, and Xie (2018) study the link between the corporate cost of capital and shareholder protection laws in the United States. On the basis of a sample of about 5,000 public firms between 1985 and 2013, they find that weakened litigation rights for shareholders increase firms' implied cost of capital by approximately 5% above the sample median.

Shareholders' rights are positively associated with economic growth. Brown, Martinsson, and Petersen (2013) find that firms with strong shareholder's rights and better access to financing from their shareholders are more likely to invest in research and development. The analysis is based on a sample of 32 high- and middle-income economies.

When lending is limited during banking crises, stock markets provide an alternative source of funds for firms. Levine, Lin, and Xie (2016) study this relationship using data for 36 economies from 1990 to 2011 and find that stock markets better mitigate the challenges of a crisis when stronger shareholder protection laws are in place. Economic crises tend to reduce firm value. Jenwittayaroje and Jiraporn (2019) find that having independent directors significantly improved firm value (by roughly 4%) during the recession of 2008. Cremers and Ferrel (2014) find a robustly negative association between restrictions on shareholder rights and firm value using data from the United States.

Tax regulation

Using data from Pakistan for the 2006–11 period, Waseem (2018) finds that following a tax increase firms react by underreporting profits, moving to the informal economy, or changing their legal form. Also, even though tax revenue was higher immediately after the tax increase, three years later it was below initial levels.

Belitski, Chowdhury, and Desai (2016) investigate the interaction between corruption and corporate income tax rates across a panel of 72 economies in the period 2005–11 and find that higher tax rates consistently discourage entry. They also find that corruption offsets the negative influence of high taxes on entry. Rocha, Ulyssea, and Rachter (2018) find that reducing taxes once registration costs have been eliminated reduced firm informality in Brazil; however, this effect comes mainly from the registration of existing firms and not from the creation of new formal businesses.

Harju, Matikka, and Rauhanen (2019) show that high compliance costs produce reactions from entrepreneurs similar to those associated with changes in tax rates (figure 2.3). Using evidence from value added tax filings in Finland, the authors find that an increase in sales is the result of a reduction in compliance costs rather than the level of the value added tax rate.

Esteller-Moré, Rizzo, and Secomandi (forthcoming) study the extent to which taxes matter in directing foreign direct investment (FDI) inflows and find that there is heterogeneity between Organisation for Economic Co-operation and Development (OECD) and non-OECD economies. Using the dataset produced by Djankov and others (2010), the authors show that taxes in non-OECD countries affect FDI flows, whereas they have no significant impact in OECD countries.

Foreign direct investment

Doing Business measures regulation from the point of view of domestic entrepreneurs. The efficiency of regulation affecting domestic firms, however, is correlated with regulation affecting FDI. Corcoran and Gillanders

FIGURE 2.3 The percentage of voluntarily registered firms in Finland increased after the reduction in compliance costs

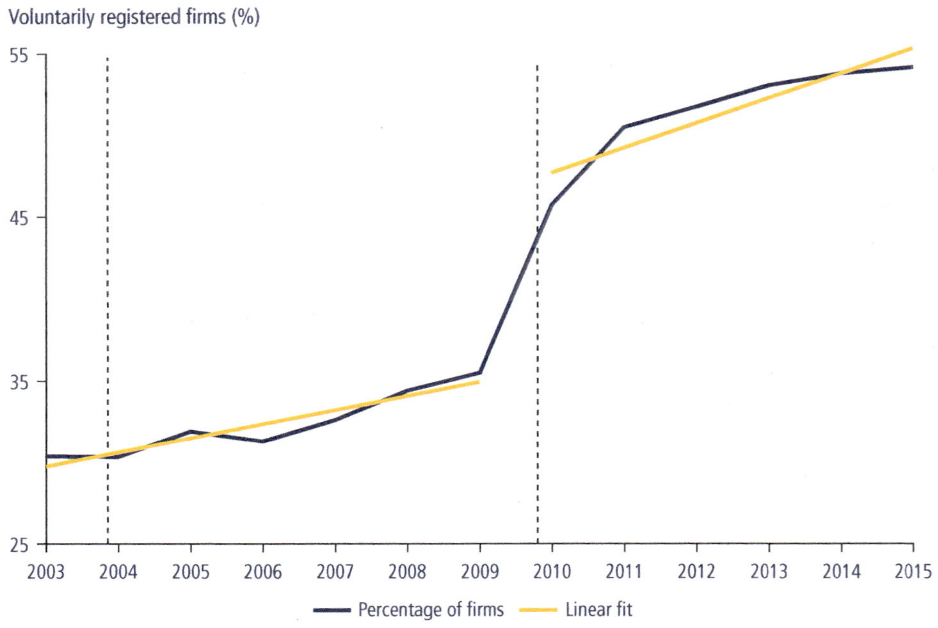

Source: Harju, Matikka, and Rauhanen 2019.

Note: Value added tax registration is defined separately for each entrepreneur in each year. The vertical line before 2004 shows the tax rate reform introducing a VAT relief scheme. The line before 2010 shows the year where the reduction in compliance costs occurs.

(2015) study this connection and find a strong correlation between foreign investment and the ease of doing business ranking for the period 2004–09. They also find that this result is primarily driven by the *Doing Business* ease of trading across borders component.

Munemo (2014) also studies this connection using data for 138 economies over the period 2000–10. The study finds evidence that foreign investment crowds out domestic investment in economies with entry regulation costs above a certain level. This evidence suggests that reforming business start-up regulation plays a role in enhancing the complementarity between foreign and domestic business activity.

The complexity of tax systems is a major determinant of FDI. Lawless (2013) studies this relationship using data from 16 high-income source economies and 57 host economies. The author finds that the number of payments and time to comply with tax obligations have significant negative effects on whether foreign investment flows are present. Specifically, a 10% reduction in tax complexity is comparable to a 1% reduction in the effective corporate tax rate.

Overall business regulatory environment

The *Doing Business* indicators correlate with different outcomes of interest to policy makers. Kraay and Tawara (2013) evaluate this relationship with data for all *Doing Business* topics and all economies and find that quantifying the partial effects of indicators on relevant outcomes is challenging. Using data for 189 economies for the period 2005–13, however, Djankov, Georgieva, and Ramalho (2018) find that business-friendly regulation is correlated with a lower poverty head count at the economy level. This association is significant using *Doing Business* data on getting credit and enforcing contracts. Additional analysis suggests that the conduit for poverty reduction is business creation, both as a source of new jobs and as a manifestation of thriving entrepreneurship.

Summary

Changes that improve regulatory efficiency have positive effects on entrepreneurship, firm formalization, access to credit, and FDI.

Still, questions remain. First, what is the complementarity of different regulatory reforms? *Doing Business* data tell us which reforms politicians make together. Research needs to tell us whether this is the right combination of reforms for improved economic and social outcomes. Second, how do some economies reform regulation consistently over an extended period? In other words, does democracy—and frequent changes in government—incentivize more or less reform? Finally, what is the profile of the reformers: young or more experienced politicians, officials facing economic crises or an extended period of stability? The answers to such questions may teach us about the logic of regulatory reform.

Notes

1. Based on searches for citations in the nine background papers that form the basis of the *Doing Business* indicators in the Social Science Citation Index and Google Scholar (http://scholar.google.com).
2. The exception to this rule is Djankov, McLiesh, and Ramalho (2006) because they examine the impact of overall business regulation on economic growth.
3. For example, a difference in trial length between the 5th and 95th percentile is associated with a difference of almost 60% in job turnover.
4. Favara and others (2017), however, find that, for distressed firms in particular, imperfect enforcement of debt contracts in default reduces shareholder-debtor conflicts and induces leveraged firms to invest more and take on less risk as they approach financial distress.

CHAPTER 3

Removing obstacles to entrepreneurship

- Fifty-eight economies have eliminated the need for paid-in minimum capital to start a business, whereas 48 others have reduced the amount of capital required.
- Fifty-six new credit bureaus and 32 new credit registries have launched worldwide.
- Sixty-three economies have introduced online systems for filing and paying taxes.
- Forty-five economies have adopted reforms implementing or strengthening reorganization procedures to resolve insolvency.

Doing Business has recorded more than 3,800 regulatory reforms since the first study was published in 2003. Many of those reforms were implemented in four areas measured by *Doing Business*—starting a business, getting credit, paying taxes, and resolving insolvency.

Uruguay provides an example of the challenges faced by entrepreneurs and firms as well as of the improvements resulting from reforms. In 2003, entrepreneurs in Uruguay were required to deposit capital blocked at the bank equivalent to 212% of income per capita, making it expensive to start a business. Paying taxes was cumbersome for firms, with an average of 55 payments taking 304 hours to complete each year. With limited access to credit—and a low asset recovery rate in cases of bankruptcy—operating a business was challenging. Today, entrepreneurs in Montevideo decide what capital they need when they start a business. Thanks to the introduction of online tax services, the number of tax payments has been cut by one-third and the time to pay by half. With 100% of the adult population covered by a credit bureau, access to credit has been strengthened. And, if things go wrong for the company, entrepreneurs can attempt a reorganization. As a result, the recovery rate for firms in Uruguay improved significantly, rising from 12 to 45 cents on the dollar.

Starting a business: Eliminating paid-in minimum capital requirements

In *Doing Business 2004*, 124 economies required fixed paid-in minimum capital to start a business. By 2019, this number has fallen by half, with many governments eliminating the requirement after it failed to serve its intended purpose of protecting creditors.

Origins of paid-in minimum capital requirements: Controlling who can start a company

Paid-in minimum capital is the amount that entrepreneurs must legally deposit in a bank or with a notary when incorporating a business. In 1855, members of the United Kingdom's House of Lords were among the first to mention a minimum capital requirement. It was initially proposed that companies should have capital of no less than 20,000 pounds sterling in the context of the railway mania.[1]

Paid-in minimum capital requirements appeared elsewhere in Europe in the second half of the 19th century. Entrepreneurs were required to obtain government permission to start a company until the mid-1800s, and the required concessions involved considerable government scrutiny. Following the removal of concession prerequisites, European economies experienced a boom in business creation and, in some cases, speculation in the railway industry and banking sector. In response, governments enacted new regulation with stricter rules to start a business.

In Germany, for example, the Corporations Act of 1870 created the concept of joint-stock companies, which required entrepreneurs to comply with more onerous rules when setting up a company, including much larger share values.[2] The act specified a minimum value per share of 50 German thalers for named shares and 100 thalers for bearer shares. A fixed nominal paid-in minimum requirement to start a company was first introduced in the 1892 law on limited liability companies.[3] Such firms were required to have an issued capital of at least 20,000 marks, of which at least 25% had to be paid in before the firm could operate. This amount was substantial—with income per capita of 470 marks in Germany in 1892, the paid-in minimum capital requirement was the equivalent of 42 times income per capita.[4]

Other European economies also introduced nominal paid-in minimum capital requirements. Sweden, for example, passed a Companies Act in 1895 and introduced a nominal minimum share capital. Portugal passed similar legislation in 1911, Austria in 1916, and most other Western European countries by the mid-1930s—including France, Italy, and Spain. Such legislation later spread beyond Europe to economies like Brazil, Chile, and Colombia.

Toward helping business

Once viewed as a way to provide security to creditors, paid-in minimum capital requirements proved to be inefficient.[5] In some economies, entrepreneurs would borrow the amount required for deposit at the time of business registration only to withdraw it immediately after. Worse, paid-in minimum capital requirements create barriers that prevent entrepreneurs from formalizing.[6] These requirements especially affect female-owned businesses, which tend to have less start-up capital.[7]

Doing Business has tracked paid-in minimum capital requirements in 190 economies since 2003. During that period, 106 economies enacted 139 regulatory reforms reducing or eliminating paid-in minimum capital requirements. Of these, 79 economies implemented one regulatory change, and 27 economies enacted more than one. Angola, for example, made three successive reductions of the minimum capital requirement in 2003, 2006, and 2011 before eliminating it in 2016.

Fifty-eight economies eliminated paid-in minimum capital requirements. The most proactive regions were Europe and Central Asia (16 regulatory changes) and the Middle East and North Africa (12 regulatory changes). Some of the most recent examples are found among high-income economies of the Organisation for Economic Co-operation and Development (OECD). In May 2019, for example, Belgium amended its Commercial Code to abolish the paid-in minimum contribution requirement for limited liability companies. Following the reform, company founders were required only to prove sufficient equity to carry out operations in their financial plans.

Within the same period, *Doing Business* captured 81 regulatory changes reducing the amount of the paid-in minimum capital requirement. Sub-Saharan Africa was the region implementing the greatest number of reductions.

Many of these cuts were made by the 17 member states of the Organization for the Harmonization of Business Law in Africa (Organisation pour l'Harmonisation en Afrique du Droit des Affaires, or OHADA). Entering into force in May 2014, the revised Uniform Act regarding the Law of Commercial Companies and Interest Economics Associations simplified the rules for the creation of companies and allowed member states to set paid-in minimum requirements nationally, with a minimum of 5,000 CFA francs ($9) per share. The Central African Republic, for example, reduced its paid-in minimum capital requirement from 527% of income per capita in *Doing Business 2004* to 35% of income per capita in *Doing Business 2020*. Similarly, 20 OECD high-income economies introduced at least one reduction. In April 2019, Denmark lowered its paid-in minimum capital requirement from 50,000 kroner ($7,470) to 40,000 kroner ($5,975) for domestic limited liability companies. In the Europe and Central Asia region, paid-in minimum capital requirements were reduced 16 times during the last 17 years. For example, Croatia reduced its paid-in minimum capital requirement by half in April 2019, from 10,000 kunas ($1,505) to 5,000 kunas ($752).

The most significant changes, however, took place in the Middle East and North Africa (figure 3.1). The average paid-in minimum capital requirement in the Middle East and North Africa in *Doing Business 2004* was 466% of income per capita.[8] In *Doing Business 2020* it has fallen to just 5%. Jordan and Saudi Arabia made the biggest reductions over time—from over 1,000% of income per capita in *Doing Business 2004* to a zero paid-in minimum capital requirement.

FIGURE 3.1 Economies in the Middle East and North Africa cut paid-in minimum capital requirements the most over time

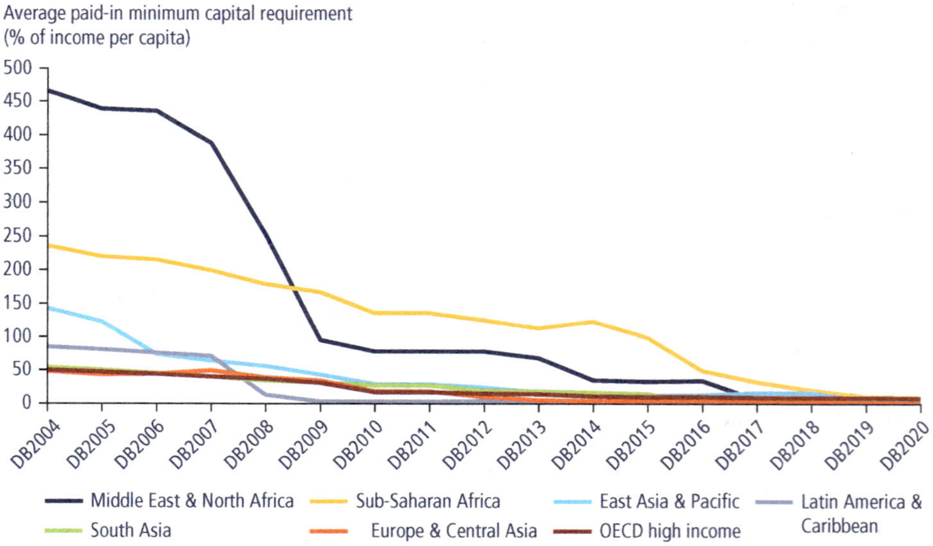

Source: Doing Business database.

Note: Myanmar and the Syrian Arab Republic were removed from regional averages as outliers.

How do paid-in minimum capital requirements relate to business formalization and viability?

When deciding to incorporate a business, founders consider several factors: what legal form the company will take, what its main activities will be, where the premises will be located, how to advertise and promote the company, and so on. With a variety of start-up expenses—from incorporation costs to purchasing materials and equipment to paying salaries—the requirement to pay in a certain minimum capital necessitates additional cash that entrepreneurs must generate and be able to set aside. These costs may negatively affect an entrepreneur's decision to start a business. Data suggest that higher requirements for paid-in minimum capital are associated, on average, with lower new business entry (figure 3.2).

Furthermore, higher minimum capital that must be paid in upon incorporation is associated with a higher percentage of firms expected to pay bribes to get an operating license and with a higher share of firms identifying access to finance as a major constraint.[9]

Early advocates of paid-in minimum capital requirements believed that they served as a protection for investors. However, *Doing Business* data show

FIGURE 3.2 The higher the paid-in minimum capital requirement for business start-ups, the lower the business entry rate in the economy

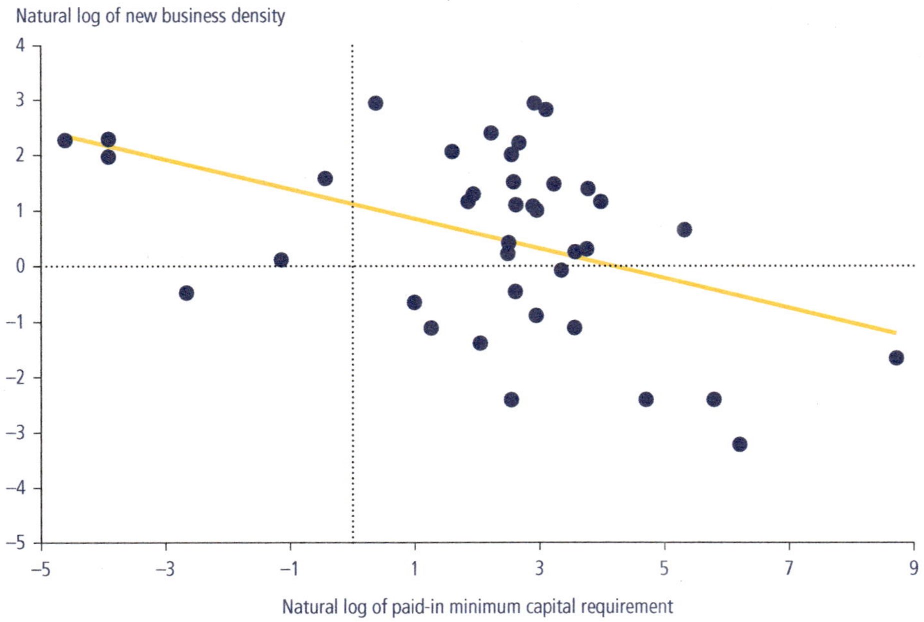

Sources: Doing Business database; Entrepreneurship database (http://www.doingbusiness.org/data/exploretopics/entrepreneurship), World Bank.

Note: The analysis was conducted using cross-sectional data as well as panel data with economy and year fixed effects regression. The paid-in minimum capital requirement reflects the amount that an entrepreneur needs to deposit in a bank or with a third party, and it is recorded as a percentage of the economy's income per capita. New business density represents the number of newly registered corporations per 1,000 working-age people (age 15–64). The relationship is significant at the 5% level after controlling for income per capita. Annual data are available for 2006–16; the dataset comprises 93 economies where observations are available on both metrics. For visual simplification, the graph displays data only for 2014 with 39 observations.

that economies requiring businesses to pay in 100% or more of income per capita upon incorporation tend to have a recovery rate that is 17 cents lower, on average, than economies that require less capital.[10] Economies with lower paid-in minimum capital requirements also tend to have, on average, stronger regulation for the protection of minority investors.[11] In the end, investor protection is guaranteed with much more efficient ways than the requirement of a fixed paid-in minimum capital for all companies.

Getting credit–credit information: Developing credit reporting systems

Since the inception of *Doing Business*, 56 new credit bureaus and 32 new credit registries have launched worldwide. Credit information sharing has become a key element in the infrastructure of credit markets around the world as a prerequisite for sound risk management and financial stability. Credit bureaus and registries offer a way to minimize the problem of asymmetric information because they help lenders better predict borrowers' capacity to repay, therefore reducing the probability of default.[12]

The emergence of credit information sharing around the world

Before the establishment of credit reporting service providers, credit information sharing took place informally. During the 19th century, communities and merchants in the United Kingdom shared only negative information, maintaining lists of individuals with poor credit records in an effort to reduce their own risk and offer credit to more borrowers. The first formal arrangement for credit information sharing emerged in the United States in the 1840s with the creation of the first commercial credit reporting registries.[13]

In the 1950s and 1960s the first bureaus operated with limited information and focused on particular industries, such as banks and retailers. Credit reporting systems have evolved from distributing only negative information (for example, individuals with overdue payments) to including positive information that allows a debtor to create "reputational collateral," typically in the form of a credit score that signals a borrower's individual creditworthiness to a large pool of lenders. Since the 1980s, the credit reporting industry has expanded worldwide.

Expanding consumer credit has fueled the emergence of credit bureaus and registries in developing economies. In recent decades, major international bureaus have opened in low-income economies, bringing their expertise developed in high-income markets.

Improving credit reporting systems in developing economies

Credit bureaus and registries have become nearly universal. Whereas 67% of economies had a private credit bureau or a public credit registry in *Doing Business 2005*, in 2019 that figure is 88%.

In *Doing Business 2005*, all OECD high-income economies had an operating credit bureau or registry compared to 57% of economies in Sub-Saharan Africa.

Since then, most new credit bureaus and registries were established in developing regions. Before 2008, Sub-Saharan Africa had very few credit bureaus and lending markets were underdeveloped.[14] Governments began passing laws licensing credit bureaus and mandating credit information sharing by commercial banks. In *Doing Business 2020*, 92% of economies in Sub-Saharan Africa have an operational credit bureau or registry (figure 3.3). Seventeen of the 62 new credit bureaus and 15 of the 39 new credit registries launched since the first *Doing Business* study were established in Sub-Saharan Africa. The Europe and Central Asia region follows closely, with 16 credit bureaus and 7 credit registries founded since the inception of *Doing Business*. Eastern European economies had no private credit bureaus until the mid-1990s and, as they transitioned to market economies, required legislative changes to encourage commercial banks to share credit data.

Despite substantial reform, Sub-Saharan Africa remains the region with the least developed credit information systems. Until recently in the economies of the West African Economic and Monetary Union (Union Economique et Monétaire Ouest Africaine, or UEMOA) credit information was available only through the Central Bank of West African States (Banque Centrale des Etats de l'Afrique de l'Ouest, or BCEAO) credit registry, which operated with minimal features. The registry did not provide comprehensive credit reporting services to lenders; instead, its primary aim was to support the BCEAO's supervision functions. In 2015 the BCEAO selected Creditinfo VoLo as the accredited company to operate a credit bureau in its member economies; operations began in February 2016.

FIGURE 3.3 Europe and Central Asia and Sub-Saharan Africa saw the largest increases in credit reporting service providers since 2005/06

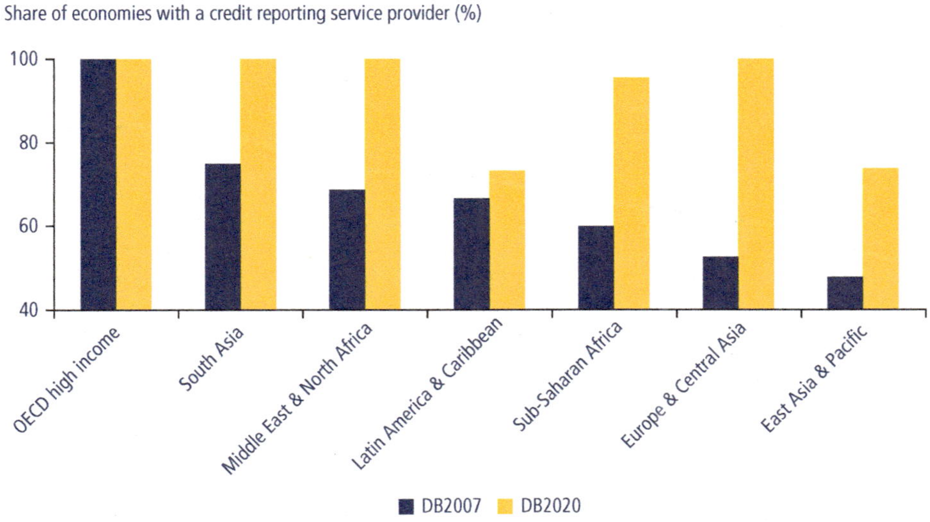

Source: Doing Business database.

Note: The sample includes 174 economies with data available back to *Doing Business 2007*.

In Nigeria, credit bureaus were formally recognized starting in 2008 when the Central Bank of Nigeria licensed three private credit bureaus. As in UEMOA economies, the low coverage rate presented an obstacle to credit bureau development in Nigeria. In 2010, the largest credit bureau, CRC Credit Bureau Limited, covered just 4.1% of the adult population and offered basic services including online distribution of positive and negative credit data on any loan amount to both individuals and firms. In 2011, two retailers started providing data to CRC, and by 2018 CRC had increased its coverage to 14% of the adult population and offered credit scoring services, thus achieving a score of 8 (the maximum score) on the depth of credit information index.

Impact of establishing new credit information systems

Doing Business data indicate that firms are 9% less likely to identify access to finance as a major constraint in economies where a bureau or registry exists. Economies with credit bureaus are also associated with higher credit-to-GDP ratios (figure 3.4).

Setting up new credit bureaus and registries has positive effects within economies. The launch of a credit bureau in Kenya, for example, has helped to reduce interest rates, collateral, and default rates for loans at commercial banks.[15] In India, lenders in the microfinance industry observed 50% lower default rates as well as higher operational efficiencies.[16]

Credit bureaus launched in 2019 are more likely to generate a higher score in the *Doing Business* depth of credit information index upon their establishment, with features including the distribution of credit scores,

FIGURE 3.4 The establishment of a credit reporting service provider is associated with more private credit in an economy

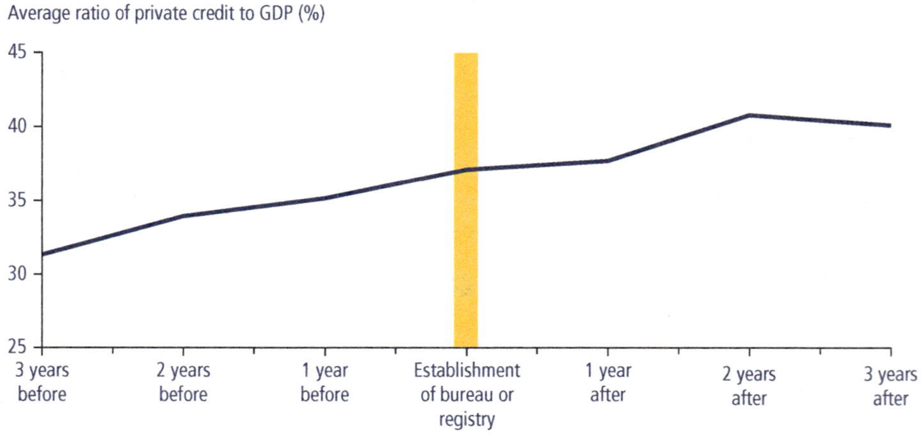

Source: Doing Business database.

Note: The analysis was conducted using ordinary least squares regression with year dummies. The figure represents an average private credit-to-GDP ratio for all economies with a credit bureau or public registry launching between *Doing Business 2006* and *Doing Business 2017*. The relationship is significant at the 1% level after controlling for income per capita and exogenous changes over time.

positive data (like on-time payment status), and data from alternative sources (such as utilities or retailers) that help to increase their coverage. Although credit bureaus opening in 2004/05 scored 2.5 points on average (out of 6 points) on the depth of credit information index, private bureaus that opened in 2017/18 scored 5 points on average.[17] In *Doing Business 2006*, it was more common for credit bureaus to launch with only a few features, such as distributing data on both individuals and firms and distributing both positive and negative data. By 2019 new bureaus and registries typically launch with the capacity to provide credit scoring services, data on utility credit, and online platforms.

Paying taxes: Transitioning from manual to electronic filing and payment

In *Doing Business 2006*, only 43 economies had an online system for filing and paying taxes. Fifteen years later, this number has more than doubled (to 106) as economies shift from manual filing and in-person payment of taxes to filing tax returns electronically and paying taxes online.

Origins of online filing of tax returns: Making compliance with tax obligations easier

Electronic filing (e-filing) and electronic payment (e-payment) are the processes of submitting tax returns and payments over the Internet. E-filing and e-payment have various benefits that have made the tax preparation process easier for businesses, including the ability to file a tax return from one's office at a convenient time and the ability to prepopulate tax returns with data already held by the tax administration.

The United States was the first economy to introduce e-filing in 1986, followed by Australia in 1987.[18] E-filing in the United States began as a small test program consisting of just five tax preparers from the cities of Cincinnati, Raleigh-Durham, and Phoenix.

Although tax preparers used special computers and software to simplify tax preparation in the 1980s, they still had to print all the forms and mail them to the Internal Revenue Service (IRS). The early e-filing process consisted of tax preparers using a machine called Mitron—a tape reader with a modem. The tax preparer would insert the tape with the tax data and then transfer it to the IRS. At the IRS, an agent would transfer the tape into a supercomputer called Zilog, which would read the data and organize it into files that the IRS could use for processing. The program's success prompted the IRS to expand it to additional cities. By 1987, 66 tax preparers from seven U.S. cities had used the system to file roughly 78,000 tax returns. To improve the system, that year the IRS added an electronic direct deposit option, allowing tax refunds to be wired to the taxpayer's bank account.

In 1988 the IRS moved to an IBM processing system, which eliminated the need for an IRS employee to manually connect a phone to a modem.

The IRS e-filing system became operational nationwide in 1990, and 4.2 million taxpayers filed their returns electronically that year. Today, in the United States e-filing and e-payment are the most common means used by taxpayers to file and pay their taxes.

From paper to electronic tax returns and tax compliance simplification

The introduction of electronic systems for filing and paying taxes has cut tax compliance times globally. The use of electronic tax filing and payment systems has risen sharply since 2004, with the most notable progress in the economies of Europe and Central Asia (figure 3.5). By 2018, the average compliance time in this region fell from 473 to 225 hours per year mainly because of the use of e-filing and e-payment in addition to simplifying and streamlining the tax systems of the individual economies. The most common feature of reform globally in the area of paying taxes was the implementation or enhancement of electronic filing and payment systems.

Since *Doing Business 2006*, 63 economies have introduced online platforms for filing tax returns including online payment modules. Europe and Central Asia and East Asia and the Pacific were the two most proactive regions introducing such systems. Among high-income economies, 97% use electronic filing or payments, whereas Sub-Saharan Africa has the lowest share of economies (17%) using such features. Factors inhibiting

FIGURE 3.5 The Europe and Central Asia region has made the most notable progress in reducing tax compliance time

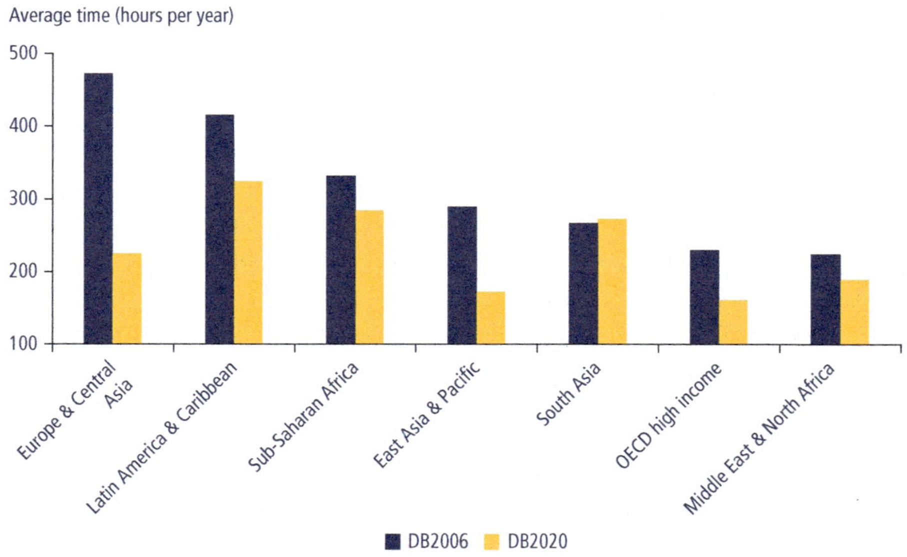

Source: Doing Business database.

Note: In South Asia, time in DB2020 is higher than time in DB2006 because of Maldives, which in *Doing Business 2013* introduced three major taxes: business profit taxes, value added tax, and pension contributions. Therefore, compliance time in Maldives went up from 0 to 391 hours.

the adoption of technology by tax administrations and taxpayers include low literacy levels, unreliable information technology (IT) infrastructure, and poor availability of suitable accounting and tax preparation software. *Doing Business* data show, however, that the use of online systems for tax filing and payment resulted in efficiency gains in several economies in Sub-Saharan Africa in 2018 including Côte d'Ivoire, Kenya, Mauritius, and Togo.

As of *Doing Business 2013*, the Czech Republic had implemented several reforms that reduced the time to file and pay taxes to just 230 hours (from 866 hours in *Doing Business 2006*). The reform process began in early 2000 with changes to regional and central tax administration organizational structures, the introduction of a mandatory tax certification test for employees, the adoption of strict tax audit guidelines, and the development of the tax administration information system. At the same time, the tax authority built a centralized tax administration register and began upgrading its systems to prepare for the transition to online tax return filing. Electronic submission of tax documentation began in 2004. Finally, in 2011, the Czech Republic expanded the list of taxpayer services provided online and established a Specialized Tax Office that launched a taxpayer–tax agency feedback mechanism to improve client services. All of these efforts resulted in a substantial reduction in the time to file and pay taxes.

China has implemented business tax reforms consistently over the years, with notable results. In *Doing Business 2006*, for example, businesses in Shanghai spent 832 hours per year on average to prepare, file, and pay taxes, and they had to make 37 payments. By *Doing Business 2020*, these metrics have been reduced to just 138 hours per year and 7 payments.

In 2014 China integrated taxpayer services functions through a mobile tax application and launched official accounts on the two main Chinese social media platforms (WeChat and Weibo). In 2015, the Internet+Taxation Initiative unlocked the potential of big data for taxpayer services, such as data sharing among government bodies, online training, and e-invoices. The State Taxation Administration launched the Golden Tax III system in 2017, which facilitated e-filing of different stamp duty taxes. Additionally, China implemented a series of measures in the past two years, which simplified corporate income tax, labor taxes, value added tax declarations, and e-delivery of invoices.

How do e-filing and e-payment of taxes relate to less corruption?

Studies show that high tax compliance costs are associated with larger informal sectors, more corruption,[19] and less investment.[20] The modernization of IT infrastructure increases efficiency, reduces physical interactions between tax officials and taxpayers, and eliminates the physical exchange of cash, which can reduce rent-seeking. Moreover, data show economies with fewer tax payments[21] have a lower perceived level of public sector corruption (figure 3.6).

Businesses care about what they get in return for their taxes. Good quality physical infrastructure is critical for the sound functioning of an economy—it

FIGURE 3.6 Fewer tax payments are associated with a lower perception of corruption

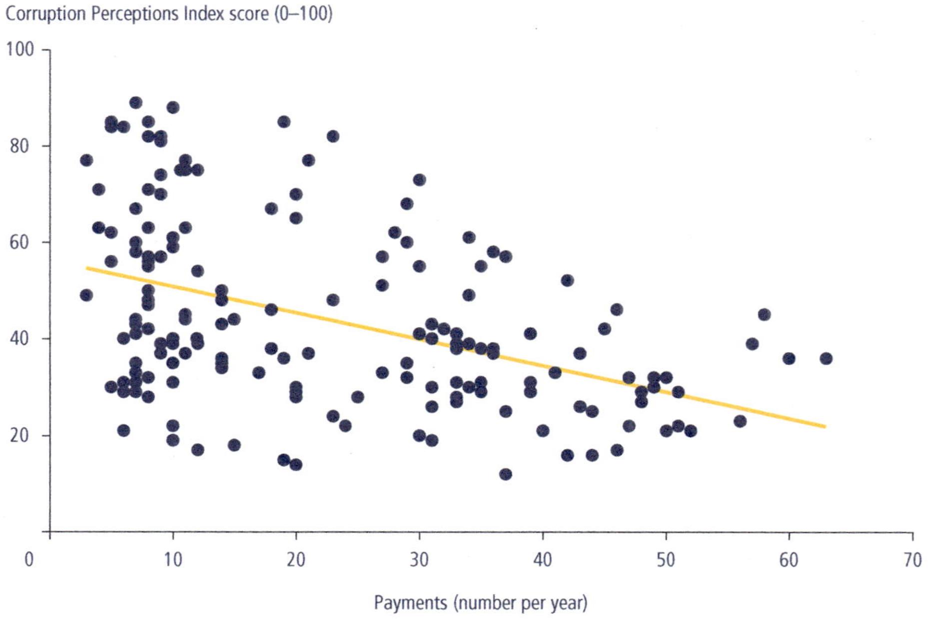

Sources: Doing Business database; Transparency International data (https://www.transparency.org/cpi2017).
Note: The figure compares the Corruption Perceptions Index with the absolute number of tax payments that a medium-size company pays in a year (for each year between 2012 and 2018). The analysis was conducted using cross-sectional data as well as panel data with economy and year fixed effects regression. The relationship is significant at the 5% level after controlling for income per capita. A higher score on the Corruption Perceptions Index indicates a lower level of perceived corruption. Data for the Corruption Perceptions Index are for 2017. The sample comprises 169 economies. In the paying taxes methodology, the number of tax payments is recorded as one when a tax is filed and paid online regardless of the statutory number of filings and payments.

plays a central role in determining the location of economic activity. The efficiency with which tax revenue is converted into public goods and services has an impact on the tax morale of businesses and individuals. Data show that, in economies where fewer tax payments result from the use of e-filing and e-payment of taxes, the public's perception of the quality of public services—and their independence from political pressure—is higher.[22] Electronic services facilitate a transparent platform for collaboration among government agencies as well as interactions with taxpayers, reducing the vulnerability of public services to political interference.

Technology is changing how taxes are administered. More and more companies are using tax software, and more and more tax authorities are creating easier-to-use online portals to simplify tax compliance. Electronic systems for filing and paying taxes benefit taxpayers by reducing preparation time and errors by enabling automated verification of transactions. These systems also benefit the tax authorities by making tax systems more robust and reducing operational costs—such as those associated with processing and handling paper tax returns—allowing human and financial resources to be reallocated to efforts that improve services to taxpayers. In the past

15 years, tax administrations worldwide have sought to introduce and continuously enhance their online systems to improve their efficiency and facilitate more comprehensive and faster risk assessment and compliance checks on returns.[23] This efficiency in turn has benefitted taxpayers by easing the compliance burden.

Resolving insolvency: Introducing or strengthening reorganization procedures

Since *Doing Business 2006*, more than 40 economies have adopted reforms implementing or strengthening reorganization procedures to resolve insolvency. Having reorganization procedures reduces failure rates of small and medium-size enterprises and prevents the liquidation of insolvent but viable businesses.

The emergence of reorganization procedures

Reorganization is a process by which the financial well-being and viability of a debtor's business may be restored through a reorganization plan, so that the business continues to operate as a going concern. In accordance with good international practices, a reorganization procedure enshrines clear rules on its commencement, including an insolvency test; provides a mechanism to manage the debtor's property; sets minimum requirements for the content and adoption of the reorganization plan; contains an element of debt restructuring; and provides a stay period for enforcement actions. Before the introduction of reorganization, corporate overindebtedness was solved primarily by applying mechanisms like in-court liquidation and schemes of arrangement with creditors.

The concept of liquidation has been present in both civil and common law economies since as early as the 16th century. Liquidation is the process of assembling and selling the assets of an insolvent debtor, emptying it and distributing the proceeds to its creditors. Liquidation rests under the assumption that exit from the market encourages entrepreneurs to reestablish themselves with a better reallocation of resources, generating firm creation and economic growth.[24] The risk, however, arises when a viable business is forced to liquidate but could otherwise become profitable with the appropriate restructuring of its obligations, management, or business industry or by undertaking other structural changes. Research also shows that after completion of liquidation, creditors often recoup only a portion of their investment.[25]

Apart from liquidation, many common law economies also still rely on other instruments like the "scheme of arrangement" for debt restructuring. Initially introduced into English law in 1870[26]—and later to the economies of the Commonwealth[27]—the scheme of arrangement is a court-approved agreement between a company and its shareholders or creditors aimed at enabling both solvent and insolvent companies to rearrange their assets and liabilities.

The scheme of arrangement is not a tool designed specifically to restore the financial viability of an insolvent business.[28] Therefore, the need for better mechanisms emerged. Modern insolvency regimes shifted the focus toward offering restructuring tools to businesses that are economically viable but face temporary financial distress, while also allowing a speedy liquidation of nonviable businesses. Inspired by commercial debt restructuring performed by merchants with their trade networks through negotiation, and supplemented with the stay of enforcement proceedings, the idea of a reorganization procedure emerged as an efficient alternative. Originally introduced into law in the United States in 1978, the first wave of reforms establishing reorganization procedures followed the financial crisis at the end of the 20th century.[29] It was at this time that legislators realized the necessity of separating unviable businesses from viable ones, and to preserve the latter. Most reforms that introduced reorganization procedures were, however, implemented during and after the 2008 financial crisis.

Introducing effective reorganization procedures is a recent phenomenon, and, in many economies, businesses facing financial distress still do not have an option to reorganize. Around the world, one-third of economies have no reorganization procedures.

Reforms introducing reorganization procedures

The case of India provides an example of successful implementation of reorganization procedures. India established an insolvency regime in 2016.[30] Before the implementation of the reform, it was very burdensome for secured creditors to seize companies in default of their loans. The most common way for secured creditors to recover the debt was through very lengthy and burdensome foreclosure proceedings that lasted almost five years, making efficient recovery almost impossible. The new law introduced the option of reorganization (corporate resolution insolvency process) for commercial entities as an alternative to liquidation or other mechanisms of debt enforcement, reshaping the way insolvent firms could restore their financial well-being or close down. With the reorganization procedure available, companies have effective tools to restore financial viability, and creditors have access to better tools to successfully negotiate and have greater chances to revert the money loaned at the end of insolvency proceedings.

Since its implementation, more than 2,000 companies have used the new law. Of these, about 470 have commenced liquidation and more than 120 have approved reorganization plans, with the remaining cases still pending. In the past, foreclosure was the most common procedure reported by legal practitioners in both Delhi and Mumbai under the case study assumptions measured by the resolving insolvency indicator set, with an approximate duration of 4.3 years. Despite some challenges in the implementation of the reform—particularly regarding court operations and the application of the law by multiple stakeholders—the number of reorganizations in India has been gradually increasing. As a result, reorganization has become the most likely procedure for viable companies as measured by *Doing Business*, increasing the overall recovery rate from 27 to 72 cents on the dollar. This increase in the recovery rate is based on the standardized methodology and underlying assumptions of the resolving insolvency indicator set, which measures domestic limited liability companies only.

Impact of reforms related to reorganization proceedings

The highest recovery rates as measured by *Doing Business* are recorded in economies where reorganization is the most common proceeding.[31] The accessibility to reorganization procedures in an economy is associated with higher lending to the private sector. Investment growth rises as a percentage of GDP as economies make reorganization procedures available, most likely because economies with faster GDP growth rates may also be able to enhance investment and vice versa. In economies without reorganization procedures, domestic investment as a percentage of GDP declined by 1% on average between 2004 and 2019; it rose by roughly 3% on average in economies where reorganization procedures are available.[32]

In those economies with reorganization procedures, domestic investment has been rising over the same period in every region except Latin America and the Caribbean. Low-income and lower-middle-income economies in South Asia and the Middle East and North Africa have been driving this trend with domestic investment growth exceeding 10%. In contrast, for economies with no reorganization procedures, domestic investment has been falling or has remained flat in every region except East Asia and the Pacific.

Notes

1. For more information, see the Limited Liability Bill of August 7, 1855, available at https://api.parliament.uk/historic-hansard/lords/1855/aug/07/limited-liability-bill#S3V0139P0_18550807_HOL_4. The Final Act, approved on August 14, 1855, omitted any requirement for minimum capital. See https://www.legislation.gov.uk/ukpga/1855/133/pdfs/ukpga_18550133_en.pdf.
2. Germany's Corporations Act of 1870 is available at http://dlib-pr.mpier.mpg.de/m/kleioc/0010/exec/books/%22158456%22.
3. Germany's 1892 law on limited liability companies (*Das Reichsgesetz betreffend die Gesellschaften mit Beschränkter Haftung, GmBH*) is available at https://www.rechtsportal.de/Rechtsprechung/Gesetze/Gesetze/Wirtschaftsrecht/Gesetz-betreffend-die-Gesellschaften-mit-beschraenkter-Haftung/GmbHG-Gesetz-betreffend-die-Gesellschaften-mit-beschraenkter-Haftung2.
4. Hoffmann, Grumbach, and Hesse 1965.
5. Dreher and Gassebner 2013.
6. Djankov and others 2002.
7. Fairlie and Robb 2009.
8. The sample excludes the Syrian Arab Republic.

9. In both cases, natural log transformation was applied to the minimum paid-in capital requirement. The analysis was conducted using panel data with economy and year fixed effects regression. For the percentage of firms identifying corruption as a major constraint, the relationship is significant at the 10% level after controlling for income per capita. For the percentage of firms identifying access to finance as a major constraint, the relationship is significant at the 5% level after controlling for income per capita.
10. The relationship is significant at the 1% level after controlling for income per capita.
11. The relationship is significant at the 1% level after controlling for income per capita.
12. Ibrahim and Alagidede 2017.
13. Lauer 2017.
14. Tchamyou and Asongu 2017.
15. Gaitho 2013.
16. Based on research carried out by High Mark Credit Information Services Private Limited in 2013–14 in partnership with the World Bank Group.
17. This calculation is based on the original methodology of the depth of credit information index on a six-point scale.
18. Che Azmi and Kamarulzaman 2009.
19. Awasthi and Bayraktar 2015.
20. Braunerhjelm and Eklund 2014; Djankov and others 2010.
21. In the paying taxes methodology, the number of tax payments is recorded as one when a tax is filed and paid online regardless of the statutory number of filings.
22. See previous note.
23. EY global survey, VAT/GST electronic filing and data extraction, 2014, available at: https://www.ey.com/Publication/vwLUAssets/EY_-_VAT-GST_electronic_filing_and_data_extraction/$FILE/EY-vat-gst-electronic-filing-and-data-extraction.pdf.
24. Asturias and others 2017.
25. Madaus 2017.
26. The scheme of arrangement was initially introduced to English law in the Joint Stock Companies Arrangement Act of 1870.
27. Payne 2014.
28. Payne 2013.
29. Reorganization procedures were first introduced in the United States Bankruptcy Code of 1978.
30. The government of India adopted the Insolvency and Bankruptcy Code 2016, which was published in the official gazette on May 28, 2016.
31. Recovery rates are calculated by *Doing Business* as cents on the dollar recovered by secured creditors in resolving insolvency.
32. The sample includes the 155 economies covered by the World Bank's World Development Indicators database.

CHAPTER 4

Employing workers

- Nearly 40% of low- and lower-middle-income economies prohibit the use of fixed-term contracts for permanent tasks. In many of those economies, such legislation is obsolete.
- Six economies revised legal restrictions on nonstandard working hours in 2018/19.
- In economies with flexible employment regulation, more young women join the labor force.

Employment laws—introduced in response to market failures including worker exploitation, discrimination in hiring and working policies, and unfair dismissal practices—are vital to worker well-being. At the same time, firms should also be free to conduct their business in the most efficient way possible. When labor regulation is too cumbersome for the private sector, economies experience higher unemployment—most pronounced among youth and female workers.[1] With fewer formal job opportunities, workers turn to the informal sector.[2] Flexible labor regulation provides workers with the opportunity to choose their jobs and working hours more freely, which in turn increases labor force participation.[3]

For example, if France were to attain the same degree of labor market flexibility as the United States, its employment rate would rise by 1.6 percentage points, or 14% of the employment gap between the two countries.[4] When Sweden increased labor market flexibility, by giving firms with fewer than 11 employees the freedom to exempt two workers from their priority list, labor productivity in small firms increased 2–3% more than it did at larger firms.[5]

Governments face the challenge of striking a balance between worker protection and labor market flexibility. As argued in the World Bank's *World Development Report 2019: The Changing Nature of Work*, extending protection is the task of the government, not the firm.[6] The employing workers indicator set measures the flexibility of employment regulation. The indicators follow the life span of a typical employment relationship—from hiring to work scheduling and eventually to redundancy in a manner consistent with international conventions.[7]

Who regulates employment the most?

Low- and lower-middle-income economies tend to regulate employment more than do high- and upper-middle-income economies (figure 4.1). For example, regulation in the Central African Republic, Madagascar, and Senegal presents significant obstacles for employers hiring new workers or dismissing redundant ones. Among lower-middle-income economies in East Asia and the Pacific, Indonesia is one of the economies with the most rigid employment regulation, particularly on hiring. In the same region and income group, Mongolia allows the use of fixed-term contracts for permanent tasks with no limit on their renewal. In the Europe and Central Asia region, regulation on hiring in Serbia is relatively rigid, and authorities could benefit from the experience of Hungary where employers have the freedom to use fixed-term contracts of up to five years for tasks of a permanent nature.

Many high- and upper-middle-income economies, including Denmark, Namibia, and the United States, have flexible labor regulation. In other advanced economies, including Luxembourg, Slovenia, and Spain, strict labor rules make the process of hiring employees arduous. Research shows

FIGURE 4.1 Low- and lower-middle-income economies regulate employment the most

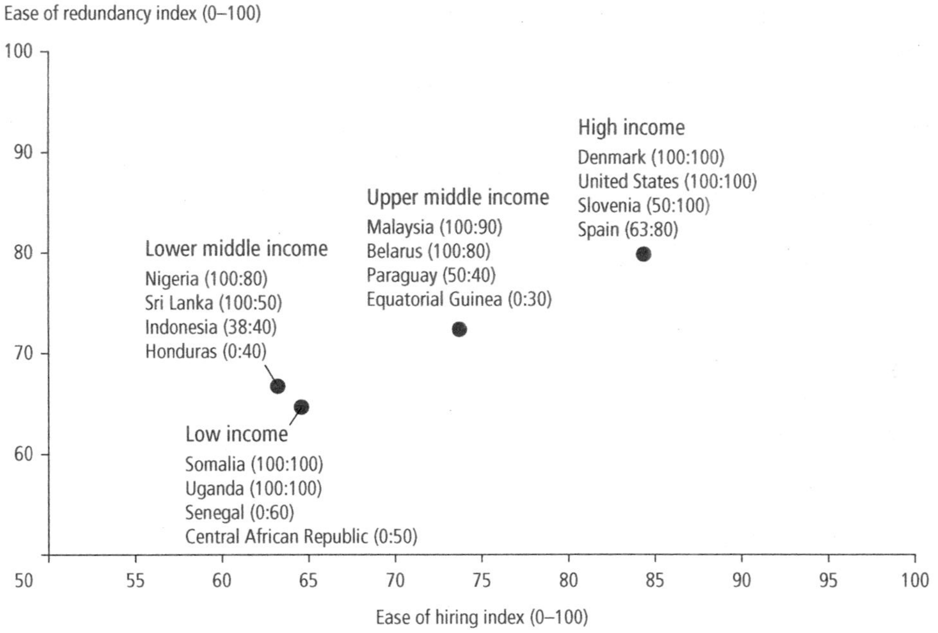

Source: Doing Business database.

Note: A higher index score indicates more flexible regulation, with 100 being the highest possible score. The dots indicate the income group average score. The numbers indicate the economy's score on the employing workers ease of hiring index (left number) and the ease of redundancy (right number). Computation of the indexes is primarily based on the *Doing Business 2013* data notes.

that strict employment protection legislation shapes firms' incentives to enter and exit the economy, which in turn has implications for job creation and economic growth.[8] When designing labor laws—specifically those that regulate hiring, work scheduling, and redundancy—authorities must assess the impact on firms.

Ease of hiring

Businesses need flexibility in hiring. *Doing Business* uses the ease of hiring index to measure the availability and maximum length of a fixed-term contract for a task related to the permanent activities of a firm, the probationary period, and the ratio of the minimum wage to value added per worker. Using a fixed-term contract, an employer can hire a worker for a specific period of time. These contracts afford employers the flexibility to respond quickly to changes during the course of their operations, temporarily substitute workers on leave, and reduce the risk of new business ventures. Fixed-term contracts can be critical to boosting youth employment by acting as a channel for youth to gain work experience.[9] *Doing Business* data show that 124 economies allow fixed-term contracts for permanent tasks. Those that do not are primarily low- and lower-middle-income economies where legislation is obsolete in this area. Honduras, for example, prohibits the use of fixed-term contracts for permanent tasks according to legislation from 1959. Pakistan limits employer flexibility in this area with legislation dating to the 1960s.

Some economies have reformed their laws governing the use of fixed-term contracts. In 2017, as part of a revision of its Labor Code, Nepal introduced fixed-term contracts for permanent tasks, and Benin made fixed-term contract renewal unlimited. Although studies suggest that potential risks could be associated with an overreliance on fixed-term contracts, the availability of fixed-term contracts should be considered in economies that have large youth populations but outdated legislation.[10]

The probationary period is used to evaluate a potential full-time employee's suitability for a job, including that person's skills, expertise, and productivity. It is a low-risk mechanism for employers, on the one hand, because it gives them the freedom to terminate employment contracts at a low cost if a worker turns out to be a poor match for the job.[11] Employees, on the other hand, use the probationary period as a means to secure a permanent job. Often the duration varies between different groups of workers, with longer average probationary periods allowed for high-skilled workers. Moldova's labor code, for example, establishes a six-month probationary period for employees in a managerial role and a one-month probationary period for low-skilled employees. The duration of a probationary period also depends on firm size. In Australia, firms with 15 employees or more are allowed to offer a maximum of 6 months of trial period, whereas firms with 14 or fewer employees can employ workers on a probationary basis for the first 12 months of their employment.

A mandatory minimum wage is designed to ensure that all workers receive fair compensation. Research shows that firms in developing economies struggle to pay minimum wages to their workers because the ratio of minimum wages to median earnings is too high relative to the ratio in high-income economies.[12] For example, a 10-percentage-point increase in the minimum wage in Indonesia was associated with a 0.8-percentage-point decrease in employment on average in a given province.[13] Turkey's subsidy for low-income workers failed to boost either employment or economic activity and negatively affected the fiscal accounts.[14] The relationship between minimum wage and employment is sometimes positive, however. A 2018 study on Mauritius—where the minimum wage is set by sector—found that a 10% increase in the minimum wage has a slightly positive effect on employment in the covered sector.[15]

Flexibility of hours

To capture the flexibility in legislation governing working hours, the employing workers indicator set measures the length of the workweek, restrictions and premiums on nonregular working hours (such as night work, weekly holiday work, and overtime work), and the length of paid annual leave. Research shows that greater employee freedom in choosing working hours leads to higher productivity.[16] Nevertheless, daily hours must not be set so high that workers become susceptible to fatigue and reduced productivity.[17] Ninety percent of economies have a workweek that is between five and a half and six days. In 2018/19 Austria and Hungary reformed in the area of working hours. Austria increased overtime to 12 hours per day and 60 hours per week.[18] Hungary raised its overtime allowance to a maximum of 400 hours per calendar year. In 2016, Hungary also removed restrictions on working hours for retail stores, allowing them to open on Sundays.

Paid leave is the period during which workers take time away from their job while continuing to receive an income and social protections.[19] *Doing Business* measures annual leave days for workers with 1, 5, and 10 years of tenure. With 23.4 working days on average, the Middle East and North Africa is the region with the most paid annual leave, followed by Sub-Saharan Africa with 21.7 days. Workers in Guinea, Libya, and Togo, for example, are entitled to annual leave of 30 working days on average, one and a half times the global average of 18.8 days (figure 4.2). However, 9 out of every 10 employees in Sub-Saharan Africa operate in the informal sector;[20] therefore, the intended social protection provided by paid leave reaches only a select few.

FIGURE 4.2 Economies in the Middle East and North Africa and Sub-Saharan Africa have the longest paid annual leave

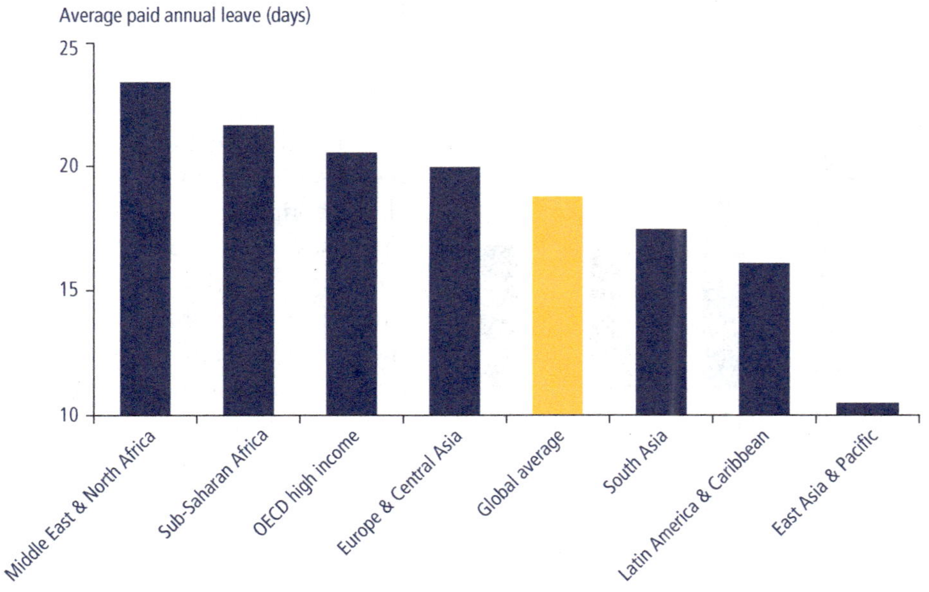

Source: Doing Business database.

Note: Paid annual leave is measured in working days.

Ease of redundancy

Cumbersome redundancy procedures pose challenges to firms. The employing workers indicator set measures aspects of regulation governing notification and approval requirements, retraining obligations, and priority rules for dismissal and reemployment. Rigid regulation can lead to a misallocation of company resources, providing older workers with job stability while leaving younger, less experienced workers vulnerable.[21]

Redundancy is permitted as grounds for dismissal in all economies except Bolivia, Oman, Tonga, and República Bolivariana de Venezuela. Half of economies globally require that a third party, such as a government agency, be notified of redundancy dismissals of a single employee or group of employees. Although approval obligations are mandatory in just 16% of economies, they complicate the process. In Ghana, for example, an employer must notify the Chief Labor Officer and the trade union of the dismissal of any employee at least three months before termination—such a rule significantly reduces the freedom of employers to adjust to shocks when they arise.[22]

Priority rules for dismissal stipulate that certain workers must be laid off first on the basis of attributes such as seniority, marital status, or number of dependents. Similarly, priority rules for reemployment require that a firm first offer any position that becomes available to workers previously dismissed for redundancy before opening recruitment to a wider pool of applicants. *Doing Business* data show that priority rules are most widespread in low-income economies (70%), where young and part-time workers remain highly vulnerable in case of redundancy termination (figure 4.3). In Cameroon, an employer must establish the order of redundancy dismissals on the basis of professional aptitude, seniority, and the expenses of a worker's family. Although priority rules aim to protect workers from unfair dismissals, they make it more difficult for those workers perceived as higher-risk—including young, female, immigrant, or disabled workers—to find employment.[23] Economies including the Kyrgyz Republic and Slovenia have eliminated priority rules for reemployment and redundancies.

FIGURE 4.3 Priority rules are most prevalent in low-income economies

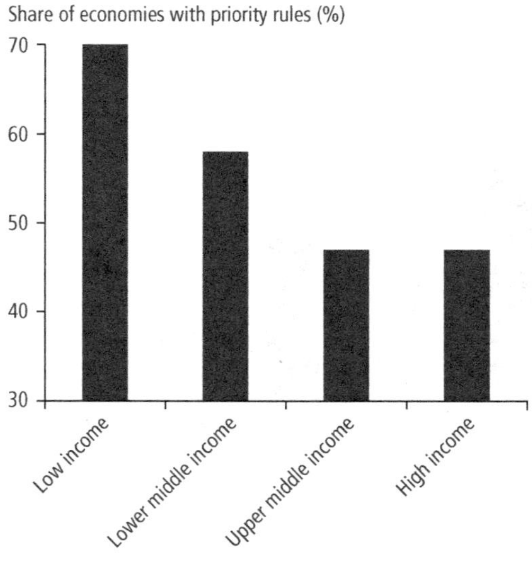

Source: Doing Business database.

Note: Data include priority rules for redundancies and reemployment.

Redundancy cost

Severance payments for redundancy dismissals aim to protect the income of redundant workers. Although the size of severance payments varies across the 79% of *Doing Business* economies that require them, they can be difficult or impossible for small firms to disburse. South Asia and Sub-Saharan Africa are the regions with the highest redundancy cost. Redundancy costs on average in South-Asia amount to more than twice the weeks of salary paid to redundant workers in the OECD high-income group. In Zambia, severance payments amount to 20 months of salary for workers with 10 years of tenure. Alternative unemployment protection systems, including unemployment benefits, can be more effective at mitigating the effects of an unanticipated worker dismissal. Whereas severance payments do not consider the worker's financial situation, unemployment insurance collects funds to provide support to workers who require support. Moreover, large severance payments rarely reach more vulnerable groups of workers. Unemployment benefit programs have been proven more effective at reaching these groups.[24]

Why flexible employment regulation matters

When faced with rigid employment protection laws, firms lose the freedom to conduct business efficiently. They find alternative ways to meet their business needs, often hiring workers informally (figure 4.4). A large informal

FIGURE 4.4 Economies with flexible employment regulation tend to have a smaller informal sector

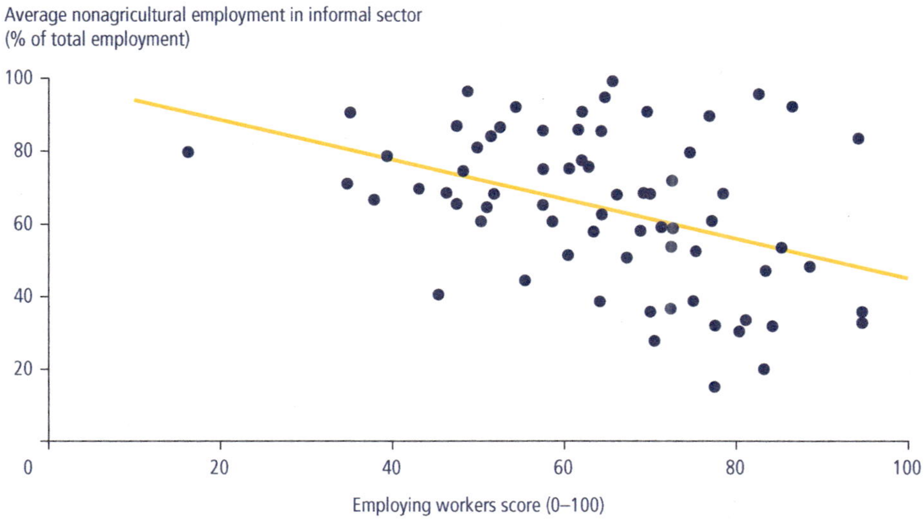

Sources: Doing Business database; World Development Indicators database (http://data.worldbank.org/data-catalog/world-development-indicators), World Bank.

Note: The figure shows the employing workers indicator set score and informal employment rate (2003–18 average). The sample comprises 68 economies. The relationship is significant at the 1% level after controlling for income per capita.

sector, particularly in developing economies, undermines productivity and economic development which, in turn, leads to increased unemployment, especially among disadvantaged groups.[25] Unemployed workers, or those with jobs in the informal sector offering no health or social protection benefits, are less likely to come out of poverty.

Restrictive labor regulation also restrains the freedom of employees to choose their employment and working hours, which negatively affects productivity. A firm's ability to adjust to shocks is adversely affected by rigid labor regulation.[26] Moreover, firms invest less in new product creation in such an environment.[27] Restrictive steps for dismissing workers cause managers to divert their attention from performing more productive tasks and investing time in innovation as well as research and development.[28] They also result in smaller firm size and the relocation of firms to economies with flexible regulation, which in turn reduces the benefits of trade liberalization.[29]

Summary

Although labor laws provide essential protections to workers, firms should not have to confront overly burdensome regulation. By changing restrictive labor regulation, economies could better adjust to fast-changing market conditions and dynamic work environments, generating positive outcomes that include smaller informal sectors, increased employment, and higher growth. Reinstating the option of fixed-term contracts would boost youth employment. Similarly, miscalculated changes to the minimum wage could lead to a decline in employment. Easing redundancy procedures facilitates businesses in allocating resources more efficiently, while revising legal restrictions on nonstandard working hours allows both employers and employees to maintain competitiveness.

Notes

1. Djankov and Ramalho 2009.
2. Djankov and Ramalho 2009.
3. Cournède, Denk, and Garda 2016.
4. Di Tella and MacCulloch 2005.
5. Bjuggren 2018.
6. World Bank 2018.
7. Five of the 189 International Labour Organization conventions cover areas measured by *Doing Business*: hours of work, weekend work, holidays with pay, night work, and employee termination.
8. Bottasso, Conti, and Sulis 2016; Fernández and Tamayo 2017.
9. Cockx and Picchio 2012.
10. Duality of labor markets can have a number of negative outcomes. For a discussion, see *Doing Business 2017*.
11. Marinescu 2009.

12. Ahn and others 2019.
13. Ahn and others 2019.
14. Betcherman, Daysal, and Pagés 2010.
15. Asmal and others 2018.
16. Collewet and Sauerman 2017.
17. Pencavel 2014.
18. As stipulated in Austria's Working Time and Rest Periods Act.
19. According to International Labour Organization Convention 132 on holidays with pay, employees have the right to take up to three weeks of paid annual leave each year.
20. Choi, Dutz, and Usman 2019.
21. Francis and others 2018.
22. As stipulated in section 65 of Ghana's Labour Act of 2003 (Act 651).
23. Kugler and Saint-Paul 2004.
24. World Bank 2018.
25. Botero and others 2004; Djankov and Ramalho 2009; La Porta and Shleifer 2014.
26. Almeida and Carneiro 2009.
27. Kleinknecht, van Schaik, and Zhou 2014.
28. Lisi and Malo 2017.
29. Almeida and Carneiro 2009.

CHAPTER 5

Contracting with the government

- Efficiency in public procurement ensures better use of taxpayer money.
- Awarding a simple contract for road maintenance takes as little as 161 days in the Republic of Korea or as long as 15 months in Chile.
- Resolving complaints raised during the award and execution of a contract takes 330 days in the Czech Republic or more than four years in the Dominican Republic.

In 2007 the Nigerian government awarded a contract for the rehabilitation of a local road. The works were slated to begin in 2009, but the project specifications had been designed six years before the contract was awarded. By the time the contractor started the works, the condition of the road had deteriorated significantly. The project was awarded at less than 60% of the cost required to execute it. At the expiration of the contract period in June 2012, the project was only 8% complete.[1] A decade after the contract award, rehabilitation works were still underway and a trip that would typically take one hour took four.[2]

Delays and cost overruns are not the only results of nonfunctioning public procurement. The waste of taxpayer money is the worst consequence. Bribes also abound. In Honduras, the now-defunct highway fund, Fondo Vial, awarded contracts to businesses run by a drug cartel to conduct road maintenance in exchange for bribes.[3]

The contracting with the government indicator set—*Doing Business*'s latest area of research—benchmarks the efficiency of the entire public procurement life cycle, with a focus on the infrastructure sector.

Why does efficient public procurement matter?

Public procurement is the process by which governments purchase goods and services from private firms. In many sectors—for example, transport, infrastructure, and education—public authorities are the principal buyers. Worldwide, public procurement accounts for between 10% and 25% of GDP on average, and governments cumulatively spend $10 trillion on public contracts each year.[4] In OECD member economies, public procurement accounts for 12% of general government expenditures.[5] At 15%, low-income economies' share of public procurement in GDP is the largest.[6] Significant variation exists among economies: the ratio of government expenditure to GDP in Finland and the Netherlands is about 20%, whereas in Bahrain and Oman it is about 7%.[7]

Inefficient procurement regulation leads to substantial losses of public funds. Studies indicate that excess costs for a public procurement project are in the range of 25–50%.[8] Research on the Democratic Republic of Congo, Indonesia, Japan, and Turkey shows that improved competition reduces prices.[9] Similarly, a World Bank study finds that higher accountability leads to lower costs in road construction projects, as do transparency in advertising and tendering in Italy and the Slovak Republic.[10] Competition also deters bribes. A study of 34,000 firms in 88 economies shows that, in economies with more transparent procurement law, firms report paying fewer and smaller bribes to public officials.[11]

Losses from bribery (that is, when a firm bribes a public official to obtain a contracting advantage) represent on average between 4% and 10% of global procurement spending.[12] A new World Bank study shows that up to one-fifth of the value of government contracts may be lost to corruption.[13] The indirect costs of corruption lead to distorted competition.

TABLE 5.1 Contracting with the government standardized case study assumptions	
Procuring entity	– Is the agency in charge of procuring construction works for the authority that owns most of the roads comparable to the one described in the contract section – Is the sole funder of the works, has budget for the works, and is solvent
Bidding company	– Is a privately and domestically owned medium-size limited liability company – Operates in the economy's largest business city – Is up to date with all regulations and is in good standing with all relevant authorities, including those related to taxes – Has all licenses and permits needed to operate in this technical area – Has already responded to a public call for tender and is already registered with the procuring entity
Contract	– Entails resurfacing 20 kilometers of a flat, two-lane road (not a highway and not under concession), connecting the main business city to another city within the same state, region, or province if applicable, with an asphalt overlay – Is valued at $2.5 million – Does not include any other work (such as site clearance, subsoil drainage, bridgework, or further routine maintenance)
Procurement process	– Is an open, unrestricted, and competitive public call for tender

The standardized case study

The contracting with the government indicators collect data through a hypothetical scenario. The standardized case study includes assumptions about the procuring entity, the bidding company, the contract, and the procurement process (table 5.1).

The construction sector was chosen because of its ubiquitous nature.[14] Worldwide, construction is a $2 trillion industry, representing between 5% and 7% of GDP in most economies.[15] Government investment in road transport alone accounts for 2.0–3.5% of GDP.[16] Because of construction's role in development (and its size), corruption in this sector is particularly harmful. The cost of collusion in the road sector is estimated at up to 60% of the contract value.[17] Roads and other large infrastructure projects are consistently delivered over budget and over time.[18] These overruns range from 20% above estimates in OECD member economies[19] to 135% of initial funding authorizations in some developing economies.[20]

What do the data show?

Three measures—the necessary procedures, the associated time, and the features regulated by the applicable laws—capture various aspects of each phase of the public procurement life cycle, from budgeting to payment (figure 5.1).

- The number of procedures describes a finite number of interactions between the contractor and various public agencies (the procuring entity, any governmental office issuing permits, a court, and so on).
- The number of days describes how long those interactions take.
- The legal index benchmarks which aspects of the public procurement process are regulated by law.

FIGURE 5.1 The public procurement life cycle

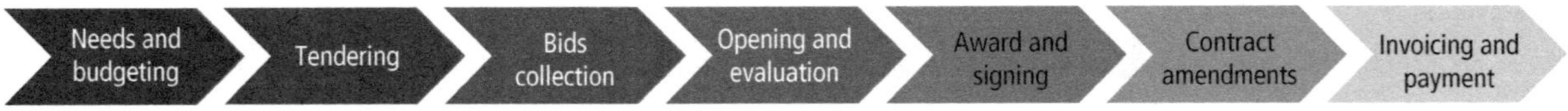

The data show vast differences in how efficient public procurement is worldwide. Sources of delay are found in every phase.

Needs and budgeting

If procuring entities do not begin the procurement cycle with a needs assessment, it is unlikely that the process will have a successful outcome. Overly optimistic budgets from faulty needs assessments result in projects delivered over budget and over time.[21]

The way the contract value is estimated varies greatly—from detailed fact-based analysis to an approximation left in the hands of public officials. In Hong Kong SAR, China, the procuring entity uses multiple instruments to value a contract, including market research to make informed decisions on design options, works implementation programs, cost estimates, and procurement method. The cost of materials is estimated through a price index established by the Civil Engineering Society, and similar projects from previous years inform other cost components. By contrast, procuring entities in Bolivia and Lebanon do not regulate which data should be used to estimate the contract value.

Another indication of planning adequacy is whether budget resources need to be secured before a procurement opportunity is advertised. In many economies, including Poland, a budget allocation is not required to proceed to the tender stage, suggesting that, when the time comes for the procuring entity to pay the contractor, funds might not be available. Others require a budget allocation that ensures that the necessary portion of the yearly budget is set aside for that particular procurement (as is the case in Canada and Slovenia, for example). Spain goes even further: in addition to requiring a budget allocation, the procuring entity must also include a document certifying the availability of funds in the tender documentation.

Budget planning matters a lot. A recent study of shortcomings in planning suggests that engineers' cost estimates are, on average, twice those provided by the funding authorization.[22] An improper needs assessment results in unnecessary purchases, waste of public funds, and excessive renegotiations.[23] The prospect of scrutiny enhances the level of attentiveness demonstrated by public officials.[24]

Tendering, evaluation, and award

At a minimum, governments need to perform the following six procedures to award a public contract:

1. Communicate the opportunity to the private sector.
2. Collect the bids.

3. Open all bids received.
4. Evaluate the bids and award the contract.
5. Sign the contract.
6. Authorize the beginning of the works.

These steps are essential to the awarding of a public contract like the standardized case study, and they take place everywhere. How rapidly they are carried out, however, as well as how many additional procedures are required, results in vast differences in efficiency. The opening of all bids received, for example, may happen immediately after the submission deadline, as in Belgium and South Africa, or may take 20 days, as in Tunisia. The time to evaluate all bids and choose the winner is about 30 days in China, Georgia, and Norway, but is more than six months in the Kyrgyz Republic and Lebanon. Additional steps, such as prequalification, take as little as 21 days in Canada or as long as 90 days in Indonesia and Pakistan, and 120 days in Ireland.

Korea—the economy in the sample that awards contracts fastest—performs the six necessary procedures in just four months on average (figure 5.2). Two additional steps are required: undergoing a prequalification process (completed in less than three weeks) and obtaining a bid

FIGURE 5.2 Time and procedures to award a public procurement contract for road maintenance in Greece and the Republic of Korea

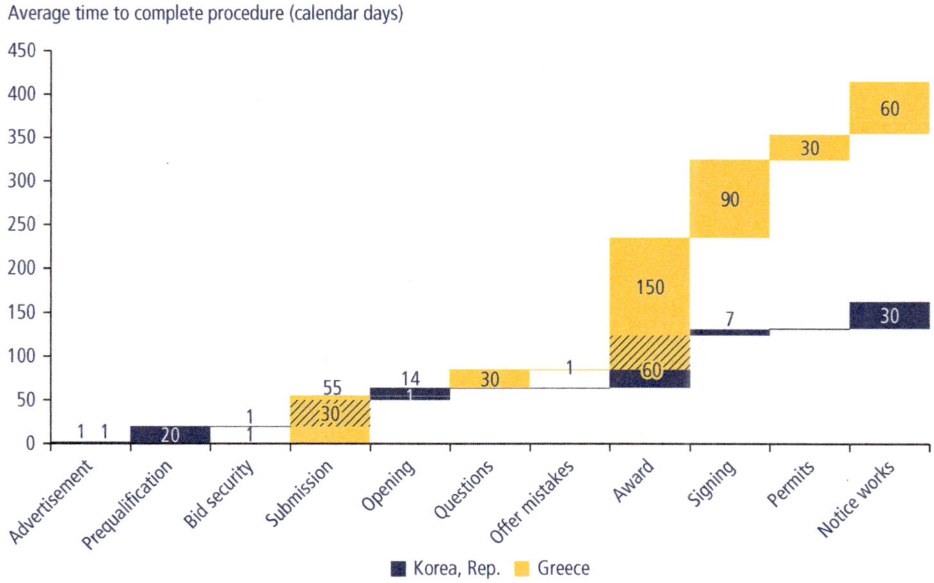

Source: Doing Business database.

Note: The number in each column refers to the number of days required for each procedure to be performed. If no number is included, that procedure does not take place in that country. In Korea, the bidding process takes 8 procedures; in Greece, it takes 10.

security (done simultaneously with the submission of the bid). All in all, awarding a simple routine contract for road resurfacing in Korea takes 161 days on average.

In other economies, the process is more convoluted. In Greece, for example, it takes one year to perform the six procedures. The deadline for submission of the bids is almost twice as long as in Korea (55 compared to 30 days). The evaluation of all bids received takes five months, and back and forth between contractors and the procuring entity typically delays it by an additional month. Once the decision is made and all documents are ready, signing the contract should take place in a matter of days. Instead, it takes an additional three months because of the need to receive approval from the Court of Auditors. Once this approval is obtained and the contract is signed, the contractor still needs to obtain an activity permit and an environmental permit before being able to commence the works—taking an additional month.

Greece grants those permits efficiently. Other economies do not. Obtaining permits to work on the road (such as occupancy permits, environmental permits, or traffic permits, if applicable) takes five months in the Arab Republic of Egypt and seven months in São Paulo, Brazil. In these economies, contractors aiming to work on government projects spend months obtaining permits from public authorities.

Efficiency in awarding public contracts improves the level of competition and encourages the participation of suppliers.[25]

Contract amendments, invoicing, and payment

Once the works begin, three procedures are necessary:

1. The contractor needs to let the procuring entity know that the works are complete.
2. The procuring entity needs to confirm that the works are indeed complete.
3. The contractor needs to receive payment.

Efficiency in carrying out these steps, however, varies tremendously. Issuing a certificate of completion report takes two weeks or less in Australia, Canada, Denmark, Finland, Hungary, the Netherlands, and Malaysia; but contractors are left waiting for more than six months in Italy. Disagreements between the procuring entity and the contractor on whether the works were properly performed may significantly delay this approval (by 320 days in Mongolia and 455 days in República Bolivariana de Venezuela, for example). The process does not end there. Despite agreement by both parties, contractors may have to wait months to obtain payment. In Lebanon, Mali, and Panama, obtaining payment takes more than six months.

Contract amendments are another source of delays during the execution of the contract. Although frequent amendments indicate poor planning, how well the procuring entity handles such amendments is an indication of efficiency. A simple change order, such as for example a change in materials that had been provided for in the initial procurement document, delays execution of the works by as little as two weeks in Canada and Finland, or as long as four months in Armenia. A more significant renegotiation of one or more contract terms delays the process by 135 days in Mexico City, Mexico, or 180 days in Tanzania. More efficient economies handle this unexpected occurrence in three weeks (as in Finland and Korea). All in all, delays in contract execution vary widely across the world. In Ireland, this phase takes five procedures and 153 days, whereas in Mozambique it takes eight procedures and 716 days.

Changes in contract terms and values are the most common channels of corruption in public procurement.[26] When the work is complete, low-quality goods are used to defraud procuring entities.[27] The delivery of substandard (overpaid) works—or a failure to deliver them at all—represents the most significant risk of this phase. Occasionally, before the delivery of subpar goods is detected, officials in the procuring entity may delay payment for completed works to solicit bribes.[28] A lack of transparency during the invoicing and payment phase leads to misuse of public funds.

Complaints

Complaints are claims brought against the public administration throughout the public procurement process. They are brought before or after the award and may refer to a variety of issues. A potential bidder, for example, could argue that the tender documents favor a specific bidder, or that a costly performance guarantee hinders access by small firms. An environmental nongovernmental organization could claim that the works harm a protected species, or that the tender documents do not include environmental parameters to ensure that they are executed in a sustainable manner. Once the contract is awarded, losing bidders could challenge the grounds of their exclusion or claim that the procuring entity granted special treatment to the winning bidder. In some cases, raising a complaint might be necessary to ensure fairness in the process. In others, it is used as a dilatory technique.

Trust in complaints procedures increases participation in the public procurement process, obtaining the best value for money. In turn, inefficient complaint resolution can stall the award and execution of a simple contract for years.

There is no minimum set of procedures to determine whether complaints work efficiently. Instead, the contracting with the government indicator set measures complaints brought before and after award, and focuses on who brings these complaints, which authority would have jurisdiction to hear them, how often they are raised, how long they would take to be resolved, and whether they suspend the procurement process.

In the Czech Republic, where complaints are usually pursued until there is no further recourse available (three tiers before contract award and three tiers after), resolving these complaints takes 330 days on average (figure 5.3). Resolving the same complaint in the Dominican

FIGURE 5.3 Calendar days to resolve complaints in the Czech Republic, the Dominican Republic, and Pakistan

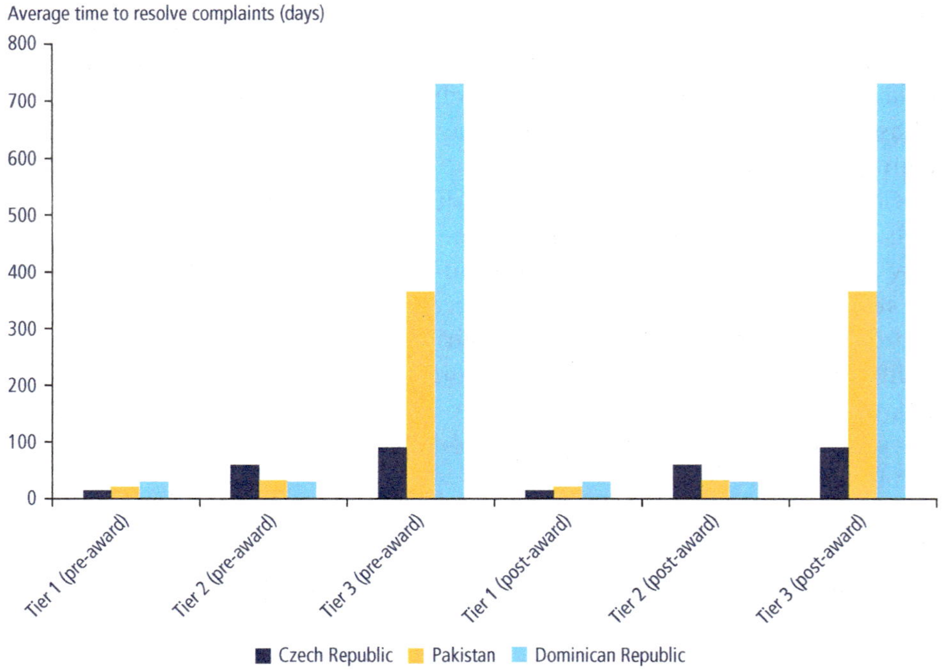

Source: Doing Business database.

Note: "Pre-award" refers to any challenge raised before the contract is awarded, such as that of a bidder arguing that the tender documents favor one specific company. "Post-award" refers to any challenge raised after the contract is awarded, such as by a bidder arguing that one of the evaluation criteria was used arbitrarily by the procuring entity to reduce the bidder's final score. Tier 1, tier 2, and tier 3 refer to the number of instances such a challenge would typically undergo.

Republic would take more than four years (1,580 days). Worldwide, resolving complaints takes longer when courts are involved, and tends to be more efficient once a dedicated administrative authority is in charge. In 2011, Tanzania established the Public Procurement Appeals Authority as an independent and quasi-judicial administrative body to resolve appeals from challenges against procuring entities in an efficient and specialized manner. As a result, challenges against award decisions are decided in 41 days, and challenges on tender documents are resolved in 18 days.

The public procurement process is carried out in a similar way around the world, but its efficiency varies greatly. And efficiency matters. Data show that, on average, economies with more efficient public procurement—as measured by the time it takes to award a contract, manage the unexpected during execution, obtain payment, and resolve challenges—tend to have lower perceived levels of corruption (figure 5.4).

FIGURE 5.4 Faster public procurement processes are associated with higher overall levels of transparency

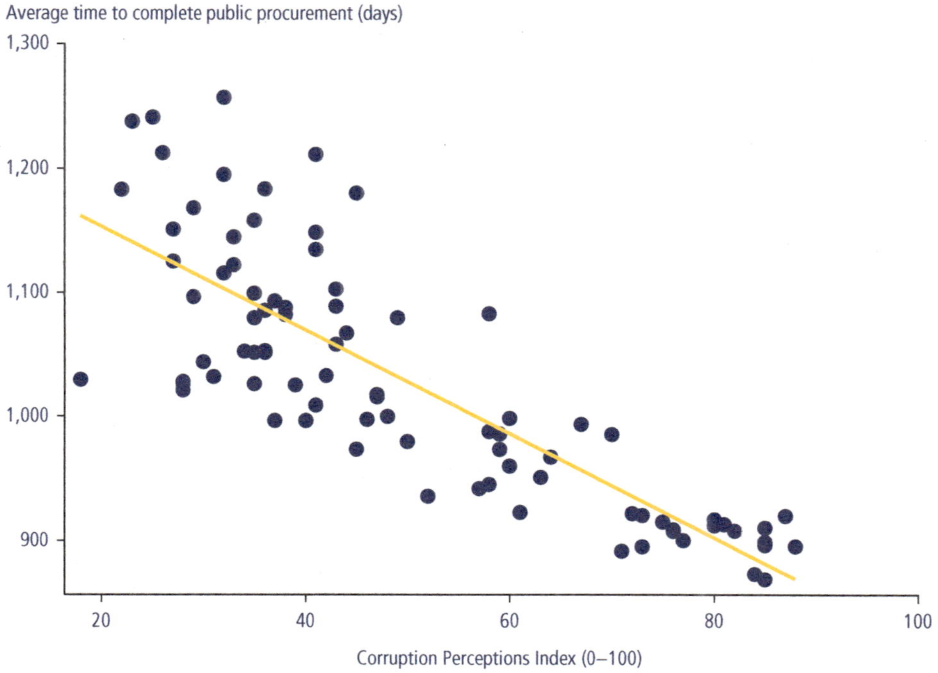

Sources: Doing Business database; Transparency International data (https://www.transparency.org/cpi2018).
Note: The Transparency International Corruption Perception Index 2018 captures perception of public sector corruption according to experts and businesspeople, using a scale of 0 (highly corrupt) to 100 (very clean). The public procurement time is recorded in calendar days. The sample includes the 85 economies for which contracting with the government data were finalized as of July 2019. The relationship is significant at the 1% level after controlling for income per capita.

Summary

The contracting with the government dataset constitutes a one-of-a-kind repository of comparable data on how the public procurement process is carried out worldwide. These data inform change. Moreover, the impact of these reforms goes beyond effective public procurement. It affects management of public funds, efficiency in their expenditure, and accountability of public officials. It also fosters innovation in the delivery of projects, potentially leading to cost savings for governments worldwide. Along with all other *Doing Business* indicators, the contracting with the government dataset will be an important tool for governments and researchers to design more efficient rules that promote growth and development.

Notes

1. Chidolue, Nwajuaku, and Okonkwo 2013.
2. Ochayi, Chris. 2016. "FG Set to Rehabilitate Enugu-Onitsha Expressway." *Vanguard*, September 19. https://www.vanguardngr.com/2016/09/fg-set-rehabilitate-enugu-onitsha-expressway/.
3. Gagne, David. 2017. "Contracts Awarded to Honduras Drug Clan Illustrate Cyclical Corruption." *InSight* Crime, March 9. https://www.insightcrime.org/news/analysis/contracts-awarded-honduran-drug-caln-illustrate-cyclical-corruption/.
4. European Commission, DG Enterprise and Industry 2014.
5. These and other OECD statistics on public procurement can be accessed at http://stats.oecd.org/Index.aspx?QueryId=78413.
6. Djankov, Simeon, Asif Islam, and Federica Saliola. 2016. "How Large Is Public Procurement in Developing Countries." Peterson Institute for International Economics (PIEE) Realtime Economic Issues Watch (blog), November 7. https://www.piie.com/blogs/realtime-economic-issues-watch/how-large-public-procurement-developing-countries.
7. Djankov, Islam, and Saliola 2016.
8. Ades and Di Tella 1997; Bardhan 1997; Rose-Ackerman 1996a; Rose-Ackerman 1996b.
9. Iimi 2006; Galletta, Jametti, and Redonda 2015; Onur, Özcan, and Taş 2012; Soraya 2009.
10. Coviello and Mariniello 2014; Pavel and Sičáková-Beblavá 2013.
11. Knack, Biletska, and Kacker 2017.
12. Auriol 2006.
13. World Bank 2012.
14. Wells 2013.
15. Kenny 2009.
16. Kenny 2009.
17. Collier, Kirchberger, and Söderbom 2015; Wells 2013.
18. Flyvbjerg, Garbuio, and Lovallo 2009.
19. Flyvbjerg, Bruzelius, and Rothengatter 2003.
20. Chong and Hopkins 2016.
21. Flyvbjerg 2017; Chong and Hopkins 2016.
22. Chong and Hopkins 2016.
23. Decarolis and Palumbo 2015.
24. Bertók 2005.
25. Kinsey 2004.
26. See red flags 8 and 9 at of the World Bank Group's "Most Common Red Flags of Fraud and Corruption" at https://www.worldbank.org/en/about/unit/sanctions-system/osd/brief/common-red-flags-of-fraud-and-corruption-in-procurement; Dudkin and Välilä 2006.
27. See red flag 10 at https://www.worldbank.org/en/about/unit/sanctions-system/osd/brief/common-red-flags-of-fraud-and-corruption-in-procurement.
28. Campos and Pradhan 2007.

CHAPTER 6

Ease of doing business score and ease of doing business ranking

Doing Business presents results for two aggregate measures: the ease of doing business score and the ease of doing business ranking, which is based on the ease of doing business score. The ease of doing business ranking compares economies with one another; the ease of doing business scores benchmark economies with respect to regulatory best practice, showing the proximity to the best regulatory performance on each *Doing Business* indicator. When compared across years, the ease of doing business score shows how much the regulatory environment for local entrepreneurs in an economy has changed over time in absolute terms, whereas the ease of doing business ranking shows only how much the regulatory environment has changed relative to that in other economies.

Ease of doing business score

The ease of doing business score measures an economy's performance with respect to a measure of regulatory best practice across the entire sample of 41 indicators for 10 *Doing Business* topics (the employing workers and contracting with the government indicators are excluded). For starting a business, for example, Georgia and New Zealand have the lowest number of procedures required (1). New Zealand also holds the shortest time to start a business (0.5 days), whereas Rwanda and Slovenia have the lowest cost (0.0). Australia, Colombia, and 118 other economies have no paid-in minimum capital requirement (table 6.1).

Calculation of the ease of doing business score

Calculating the ease of doing business score for each economy involves two main steps. In the first step individual component indicators are normalized to a common unit where each of the 41 component indicators *y* (except for the total tax and contribution rate) is rescaled using the linear transformation (worst – *y*)/(worst – best). In this formulation the highest score represents the best regulatory performance on the indicator across all economies since 2005 or the third year in which data for the indicator were collected. Both the best regulatory performance and the worst regulatory performance are established every five years[1] on the basis of the *Doing Business* data for the year in which they are established and remain at that level for the five years regardless of any changes in data in interim years. Thus an economy may establish the best regulatory performance for an indicator even though it may not have the highest score in a subsequent year. Conversely, an economy may score higher than the best regulatory performance if the economy reforms after the best regulatory performance is set. For example, the best regulatory performance for the time to get electricity is set at 18 days. In the Republic of Korea it now takes 13 days to get electricity, and in the United Arab Emirates it takes just 7 days. Although the two economies have different times, both economies score 100 on the time to get electricity because they have exceeded the threshold of 18 days.

For scores on indexes such as the strength of legal rights index or the quality of land administration index, the best regulatory performance is set at the highest possible value (although no economy has yet reached that value in the case of the latter). For the total tax and contribution rate, consistent with the use of a threshold in calculating the rankings on this indicator, the best regulatory performance is defined as the total tax and contribution rate at the 15th percentile of the overall distribution for all years included in the analysis up to and including *Doing Business 2015*. For the time to pay taxes, the best regulatory performance is defined as the lowest time recorded among all economies that levy the three major taxes: profit tax, labor taxes and mandatory contributions, and value added tax (VAT) or sales tax. For the different times to trade across borders, the best regulatory performance is defined as one hour even though in many economies the time is less than that.

TABLE 6.1 Which economies set the best regulatory performance?

Topic and indicator	Economy establishing best regulatory performance	Best regulatory performance	Worst regulatory performance
Starting a business			
Procedures (number)	Georgia; New Zealand	1	18[a]
Time (days)	New Zealand	0.5	100[b]
Cost (% of income per capita)	Rwanda; Slovenia	0.0	200.0[b]
Minimum capital (% of income per capita)	Australia; Colombia; Mauritius[c]	0.0	400.0[b]
Dealing with construction permits			
Procedures (number)	No economy was a best performer as of May 1, 2019.[d]	5	30[a]
Time (days)	No economy was a best performer as of May 1, 2019.[d]	26	373[b]
Cost (% of warehouse value)	No economy was a best performer as of May 1, 2019.[d]	0.0	20.0[b]
Building quality control index (0–15)	China; Luxembourg; United Arab Emirates[e]	15	0[f]
Getting electricity			
Procedures (number)	Germany; Kenya; Republic of Korea[g]	3	9[a]
Time (days)	Republic of Korea; St. Kitts and Nevis; United Arab Emirates	18	248[b]
Cost (% of income per capita)	China; Japan; United Arab Emirates	0.0	8,100.0[b]
Reliability of supply and transparency of tariffs index (0–8)	Costa Rica; Ireland; Malaysia[h]	8	0[f]
Registering property			
Procedures (number)	Georgia; Norway; Portugal[i]	1	13[a]
Time (days)	Georgia; Qatar	1	210[b]
Cost (% of property value)	Saudi Arabia	0.0	15.0[b]
Quality of land administration index (0–30)	No economy has reached the best performance yet.	30	0[f]
Getting credit			
Strength of legal rights index (0–12)	Brunei Darussalam; Montenegro; New Zealand[j]	12	0[f]
Depth of credit information index (0–8)	Ecuador; Israel; United Kingdom[k]	8	0[f]
Protecting minority investors			
Extent of disclosure index (0–10)	China; Malaysia; United Kingdom[l]	10	0[f]
Extent of director liability index (0–10)	Cambodia; Kenya; United Arab Emirates	10	0[f]
Ease of shareholder suits index (0–10)	Djibouti	10	0[f]
Extent of shareholder rights index (0–6)	India; Kazakhstan; Malta[m]	6	0[f]
Extent of ownership and control index (0–7)	Bahrain; Colombia; Uzbekistan[n]	7	0[f]
Extent of corporate transparency index (0–7)	France; Norway; Taiwan, China[o]	7	0[f]
Paying taxes			
Payments (number per year)	Hong Kong SAR, China	3	63[b]
Time (hours per year)	Singapore	49[p]	696[b]
Total tax and contribution rate (% of profit)	Canada; Denmark; Singapore[q]	26.1[r]	84.0[b]
Postfiling index (0–100)	No economy with both CIT and VAT has reached the best performance yet.	100	0
Time to comply with VAT refund (hours)	Croatia; Republic of Korea; Netherlands[s]	0	50[b]
Time to obtain VAT refund (weeks)	Austria; Estonia	3.2	55[b]
Time to comply with corporate income tax correction (hours)	Estonia; Lithuania; Portugal[t]	1.5	56[b]
Time to complete a corporate income tax correction (weeks)	Japan; Sweden; United States[u]	0[v]	32[b]

(table continued on next page)

TABLE 6.1 Which economies set the best regulatory performance? (*Continued*)

Topic and indicator	Economy establishing best regulatory performance	Best regulatory performance	Worst regulatory performance
Trading across borders			
Time to export			
Documentary compliance (hours)	Canada; Poland; Spain[w]	1[x]	170[b]
Border compliance (hours)	Austria; Belgium; Denmark[y]	1[x]	160[b]
Cost to export			
Documentary compliance (US$)	Hungary; Luxembourg; Norway[z]	0	400[b]
Border compliance (US$)	France; Netherlands; Portugal[aa]	0	1,060[b]
Time to import			
Documentary compliance (hours)	Republic of Korea; Latvia; New Zealand[bb]	1[x]	240[b]
Border compliance (hours)	Estonia; France; Germany[cc]	1[x]	280[b]
Cost to import			
Documentary compliance (US$)	Iceland; Latvia; United Kingdom[dd]	0	700[b]
Border compliance (US$)	Belgium; Denmark; Estonia[ee]	0	1,200[b]
Enforcing contracts			
Time (days)	Singapore	120	1,340[b]
Cost (% of claim)	Bhutan	0.1	89.0[b]
Quality of judicial processes index (0–18)	No economy has reached the best performance yet.	18	0[f]
Resolving insolvency			
Recovery rate (cents on the dollar)	Norway	92.9	0[f]
Strength of insolvency framework index (0–16)	No economy has reached the best performance yet.	16	0[f]

Source: Doing Business database.

Note: CIT = corporate income tax; VAT = value added tax.

a. Worst performance is defined as the 99th percentile among all economies in the *Doing Business* sample.
b. Worst performance is defined as the 95th percentile among all economies in the *Doing Business* sample.
c. Another 117 economies also have a paid-in minimum capital requirement of 0.0.
d. No economy was a best performer as of May 1, 2019, due to data revisions.
e. Another three economies score 15 out of 15 on the building quality control index.
f. Worst performance is the worst value recorded.
g. In 25 other economies it takes no more than three procedures to get an electricity connection.
h. Another 23 economies score 8 out of 8 on the reliability of supply and transparency of tariffs index.
i. Two more economies record one procedure to register property.
j. Two additional economies score 12 out of 12 on the strength of legal rights index.
k. Another 50 economies score 8 out of 8 on the depth of credit information index.
l. Another 10 economies score 10 out of 10 on the extent of disclosure index.
m. Another 16 economies score 6 out of 6 on the extent of shareholders rights index.
n. Another six economies score 7 out of 7 on the extent of ownership and control index.
o. Another 10 economies score 7 out of 7 on the extent of corporate transparency index.
p. Defined as the lowest time recorded among all economies in the *Doing Business* sample that levy the three major taxes: profit tax, labor taxes and mandatory contributions, and VAT or sales tax.
q. Another 30 economies have a total tax and contribution rate equal to or lower than 26.1% of profits.
r. Defined as the highest total tax and contribution rate among the 15% of economies with the lowest total tax and contribution rate in the *Doing Business* sample for all years included in the analysis up to and including *Doing Business 2015*.
s. Another eight economies also have a compliance time for VAT refund of 0 hours.
t. Another 11 economies also have a compliance time for corporate income tax correction of no more than 1.5 hours.
u. Another 96 economies also do not impose a corporate income tax correction.
v. Time to complete a corporate income tax correction is 0 when there is no audit measured for the economy. No audit is measured when the percentage of cases exposed to an additional review is less than 25%.
w. Another 23 economies also have a documentary compliance time to export of no more than 1 hour.
x. Defined as 1 hour even though in many economies the time is less.
y. Another 16 economies also have a border compliance time to export of no more than 1 hour.
z. Another 17 economies also have a documentary compliance cost to export of 0.0.
aa. Another 16 economies also have a border compliance cost to export of 0.0.
bb. Another 27 economies also have a documentary compliance time to import of no more than 1 hour.
cc. Another 22 economies also have a border compliance time to import of no more than 1 hour.
dd. Another 27 economies also have a documentary compliance cost to import of 0.0.
ee. Another 25 economies also have a border compliance cost to import of 0.0.

In the same formulation, to mitigate the effects of extreme outliers in the distributions of the rescaled data for most component indicators (very few economies need 700 days to complete the procedures to start a business, but many need 9 days), the worst performance is calculated after the removal of outliers. The definition of outliers is based on the distribution for each component indicator. To simplify the process two rules were defined: the 95th percentile is used for the indicators with the most dispersed distributions (including minimum capital, number of payments to pay taxes, and the time and cost indicators), and the 99th percentile is used for number of procedures. No outlier is removed for component indicators bound by definition or construction, including legal index scores (such as the depth of credit information index, extent of disclosure index, and strength of insolvency framework index) and the recovery rate (figure 6.1).

In the second step for calculating the ease of doing business score, the scores obtained for individual indicators for each economy are aggregated through simple averaging into one score, first for each topic and then across all 10 topics: starting a business, dealing with construction permits, getting electricity, registering property, getting credit, protecting minority investors, paying taxes, trading across borders, enforcing contracts, and resolving insolvency. More complex aggregation methods—such as principal components and unobserved components—yield a ranking nearly identical to the simple average used by *Doing Business*.[2] Thus *Doing Business* uses the simplest method: weighting all topics equally and, within each topic, giving equal weight to each of the topic components.[3]

An economy's score is indicated on a scale from 0 to 100, where 0 represents the worst regulatory performance and 100 the best regulatory performance. All topic ranking calculations and the ease of doing business ranking calculations are based on scores without rounding.

FIGURE 6.1 How are scores calculated for indicators?

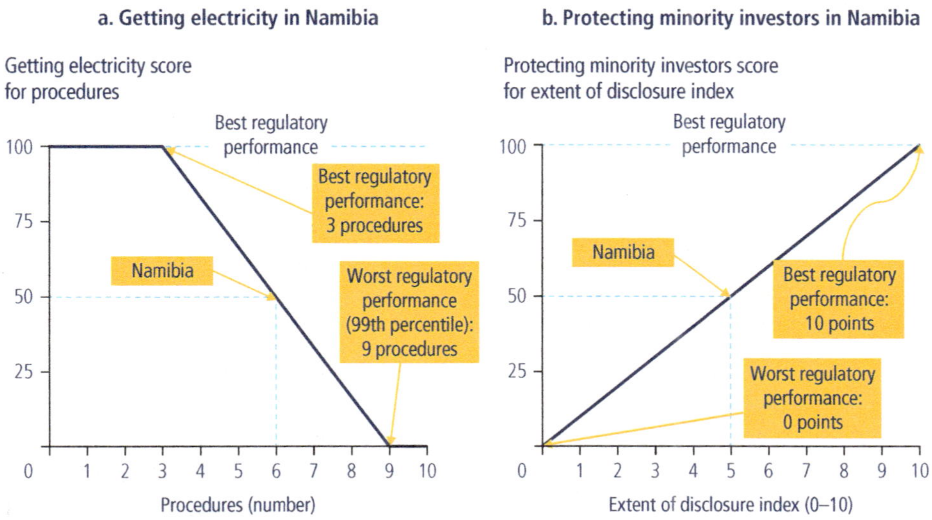

Source: Doing Business database.

The difference between an economy's score in any previous year and its score in *Doing Business 2020* illustrates the extent to which the economy has changed in its business regulatory environment over time. In any given year, the score measures how close an economy is to the best regulatory performance at that time.

Treatment of the total tax and contribution rate

The total tax and contribution rate component of the paying taxes topic enters the score calculation in a different way than any other indicator. The score obtained for the total tax and contribution rate is transformed in a nonlinear fashion before it enters the score for paying taxes. As a result of the nonlinear transformation, an increase in the total tax and contribution rate has a smaller impact on the score for the total tax and contribution rate—and therefore on the score for paying taxes—for economies with a below-average total tax and contribution rate than it would have had before this approach was adopted in *Doing Business 2015* (line B is smaller than line A in figure 6.2). For economies with an extreme total tax and contribution rate (a rate that is very high relative to the average), an increase has a greater impact on both these scores than it would have had before (line D is bigger than line C in figure 6.2).

The nonlinear transformation is not based on any economic theory of an "optimal tax rate" that minimizes distortions or maximizes efficiency in an economy's overall tax system. Instead, it is mainly empirical in nature. The nonlinear transformation along with the threshold reduces the bias in the indicator toward economies that do not need to levy significant taxes on companies like the *Doing Business* standardized case study company because they raise public revenue in other ways—for example, through taxes on foreign companies, through taxes on sectors other than manufacturing, or from natural resources (all of which are outside the scope of the methodology). In addition, it acknowledges the need of economies to collect taxes from firms.

FIGURE 6.2 How the nonlinear transformation affects the paying taxes score for the total tax and contribution rate

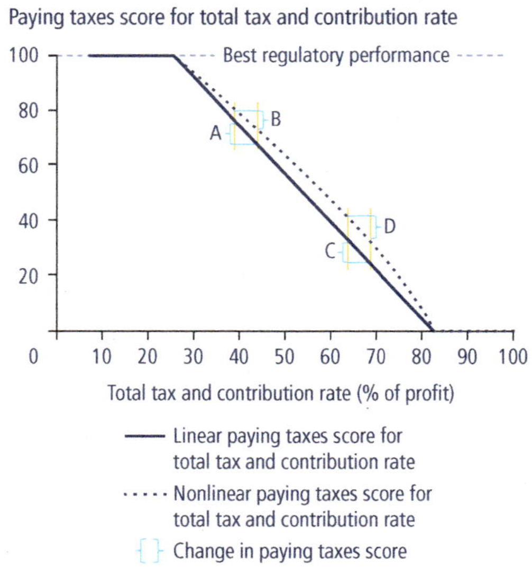

Source: Doing Business database.

Note: The nonlinear paying taxes score for the total tax and contribution rate is equal to the paying taxes score for the total tax and contribution rate to the power of 0.8.

Calculation of scores for economies with two cities covered

For each of the 11 economies in which *Doing Business* collects data for the second-largest business

TABLE 6.2 Weights used in calculating the scores for economies with two cities covered

Economy	City	Weight (%)
Bangladesh	Dhaka	78
	Chittagong	22
Brazil	São Paulo	61
	Rio de Janeiro	39
China	Shanghai	55
	Beijing	45
India	Mumbai	47
	Delhi	53
Indonesia	Jakarta	78
	Surabaya	22
Japan	Tokyo	65
	Osaka	35
Mexico	Mexico City	83
	Monterrey	17
Nigeria	Lagos	77
	Kano	23
Pakistan	Karachi	65
	Lahore	35
Russian Federation	Moscow	70
	St. Petersburg	30
United States	New York City	60
	Los Angeles	40

Source: United Nations, Department of Economic and Social Affairs, Population Division, World Urbanization Prospects, 2014 Revision, "File 12: Population of Urban Agglomerations with 300,000 Inhabitants or More in 2014, by Country, 1950-2030 (thousands)," http://esa.un.org/unpd/wup/CD-ROM/Default.aspx.

city as well as the largest one, the score is calculated as the population-weighted average of the scores for these two cities (table 6.2). This calculation is done for the aggregate ease of doing business score, the scores for each topic, and the scores for all the component indicators for each topic.

Variability of economies' scores across topics

Each *Doing Business* topic measures a different aspect of the business regulatory environment. The scores and associated rankings of an economy can vary, sometimes significantly, across topics. The average correlation coefficient between the 10 topics included in the aggregate ease of doing business score is 0.50, and the coefficients between two topics range from 0.32 (between getting credit and paying taxes) to 0.68 (between dealing with construction permits and getting electricity). These correlations suggest that economies rarely score universally well or universally badly on *Doing Business* topics (table 6.3).

Consider the example of Portugal. Its aggregate ease of doing business score is 76.5. It scores 90.9 for starting a business and 100.0 for trading across borders, but only 62.0 for protecting minority investors and 45.0 for getting credit.

Figure 1.1 in chapter 1, "About *Doing Business*," illustrates the degree of variability for each economy's performance across the different areas of business regulation covered by *Doing Business*. The figure draws attention to economies with a particularly uneven performance by showing, for each economy, the distance between the average of its highest three scores and the average of its lowest three across the 10 topics included in this year's aggregate ease of doing business score. Whereas a relatively small distance between these two averages suggests a broadly consistent approach across the areas of business regulation measured by *Doing Business*, a relatively large distance suggests a more uneven approach, with greater room for improvement in some areas than in others.

Variation in performance across topics is not at all unusual. It reflects differences in the degree of priority that government authorities give to particular areas of business regulation reform and in the ability of different government agencies to deliver tangible results in their area of responsibility.

TABLE 6.3 Correlations between economy scores for *Doing Business* topics

	Dealing with construction permits	Getting electricity	Registering property	Getting credit	Protecting minority investors	Paying taxes	Trading across borders	Enforcing contracts	Resolving insolvency
Starting a business	0.50	0.46	0.39	0.37	0.51	0.55	0.40	0.38	0.45
Dealing with construction permits		0.68	0.50	0.41	0.56	0.49	0.52	0.43	0.44
Getting electricity			0.51	0.45	0.61	0.57	0.65	0.51	0.58
Registering property				0.46	0.51	0.50	0.50	0.60	0.52
Getting credit					0.53	0.32	0.41	0.36	0.51
Protecting minority investors						0.52	0.50	0.52	0.64
Paying taxes							0.56	0.51	0.46
Trading across borders								0.49	0.54
Enforcing contracts									0.45

Source: Doing Business database.

Change in the score gap

Many topics assess the impact of data changes on the basis of the absolute change in the overall score of the indicator set and the change in the relative score gap. The change in the score gap—or the distance to the best regulatory performance—is defined as $(\text{score}^{\text{prior year}} - \text{score}^{\text{current year}})/(100 - \text{score}^{\text{prior year}})$, where "score" is the aggregate score for the specific topic. For indicators using macroeconomic variables, such as the cost of starting a business as a percentage of income per capita, the macroeconomic data for the prior year are used to control for exogenous factors such as a change in income per capita. For example, in 2018/19 Papua New Guinea reduced the time and cost to trade across borders, resulting in an improvement in its aggregate score for trading across borders from 60.5 to 65.8. This improved the overall score by 65.8 – 60.5 or 5.3 points, and reduced the score gap for Papua New Guinea by (60.5 – 65.8)/(100 – 60.5) or 13.4% on trading across borders in *Doing Business 2020*. For a complete discussion of the methodology for classifying changes as reforms, see the *Doing Business* website.

Economies improving the most across three or more *Doing Business* topics in 2018/19

Doing Business 2020 uses a simple method to calculate which economies improved the ease of doing business score the most. First, it selects the economies that in 2018/19 implemented regulatory reforms making it easier to do business in 3 or more of the 10 topics included in this year's aggregate ease of doing business score.[4] Forty-two economies meet this criterion: Armenia; Azerbaijan; The Bahamas; Bahrain; Bangladesh; Cabo Verde; China; Colombia; the Democratic Republic of Congo; Djibouti; the Arab Republic of Egypt; Eswatini; Gabon; India; Indonesia; Israel; Jordan; Kenya; Kosovo; Kuwait; the Kyrgyz Republic; Mauritius; Moldova; Morocco; Myanmar; Nigeria; Oman; Pakistan; Philippines; Qatar; the Russian Federation; Rwanda; Saudi Arabia; Serbia; Tajikistan; Togo; Tunisia; Ukraine; United Arab Emirates; United States; Uzbekistan; and Zimbabwe. Second, *Doing Business* sorts these economies on the increase in their ease of doing business score over the previous year, and the scores for both years are calculated using the same macroeconomic data (such as income per capita and currency conversion rates) to remove the effect of changes in these variables.

Selecting the economies that implemented regulatory reforms in at least three topics and had the biggest improvements in their ease of doing business scores is intended to highlight economies with ongoing, broad-based reform programs. The improvement in the ease of doing business score is used to identify the top improvers because it allows a focus on the absolute improvement—in contrast with the relative improvement shown by a change in rankings—that economies have made in their regulatory environment for business.

Ease of doing business ranking

The ease of doing business ranking ranges from 1 to 190. The ranking of economies is determined by sorting the aggregate ease of doing business scores.

Notes

1. The next update will be published in *Doing Business 2021* along with several other methodological changes such as the introduction of the contracting with the government indicators.
2. See Djankov and others 2005. Principal components and unobserved components methods yield a ranking nearly identical to that from the simple average method because both these methods assign roughly equal weights to the topics, because the pairwise correlations among topics do not differ much. An alternative to the simple average method is to give different weights to the topics, depending on which are considered of more or less importance in the context of a specific economy.
3. For getting credit and protecting minority investors, indicators are weighted proportionally, according to their contribution to the total score. The getting credit indicator weighs 60% assigned to the strength of legal rights index and 40% to the depth of credit information index. For protecting minority investors, the extent of disclosure index, the extent of director liability index, and the ease of shareholder suits index are each assigned a weight of 20%, whereas the extent of shareholder rights index

has a weight of 12% and the extent of ownership and control index and the extent of corporate transparency index each weigh 14%. Indicators for all other topics are assigned equal weights.

4. Changes making it more difficult to do business are subtracted from the total number of those making it easier to do business.

CHAPTER 7

Summaries of *Doing Business* reforms in 2018/19

Doing Business reforms affecting all sets of indicators included in this year's study, implemented from May 2018 to May 2019.

✓ Reform making it easier to do business
× Change making it more difficult to do business

Albania

✓ Getting electricity
Albania increased the reliability of power supply by rolling out a Supervisory Control and Data Acquisition (SCADA) automatic energy management system for the monitoring of outages and the restoration of service.

Reforms affecting the employing workers indicators are included here but do not affect the ranking on the ease of doing business. For reforms in paying taxes, when an economy introduces a value added tax or sales tax, the reform is classified as a neutral reform even though this type of reform increases the administrative burden on firms. The reforms in paying taxes included in *Doing Business* 2020 are those implemented in calendar year 2018 (January 1, 2018 to December 31, 2018).

Antigua and Barbuda

✓ Starting a business
Antigua and Barbuda made starting a business faster by improving the exchange of information between public entities involved in company incorporation.

Argentina

× Starting a business
Argentina made starting a business more difficult by introducing an additional procedure for legalizing the employee books for companies hiring more than 10 employees.

✓ Dealing with construction permits
Argentina made dealing with construction permits easier by streamlining procedures and implementing an electronic platform for building permit applications.

✓ Trading across borders
Argentina reduced the time required for export and import documentary compliance by introducing electronic certificates of origin and improving its import licensing system.

✓ Enforcing contracts
Argentina made enforcing contracts easier by allowing electronic payment of court fees.

Armenia

✓ Dealing with construction permits
Armenia strengthened construction quality control by imposing stricter qualification requirements for architects and engineers.

✓ Protecting minority investors
Armenia strengthened minority investor protections by requiring an independent review and immediate disclosure to the public of related-party transactions, increasing shareholders' rights and role in major corporate decisions, and clarifying ownership and control structures.

✓ Paying taxes
Armenia made paying taxes easier by extending value added tax cash refunds to cases of capital investment.

✓ Trading across borders
Armenia made exporting faster by allowing the online submission of customs declarations.

Australia

✓ Getting credit
Australia improved access to credit information by beginning to distribute both positive and negative data.

Austria

Employing workers
Austria changed regulations pertaining to working time.

Azerbaijan

✓ Registering property
Azerbaijan made registering property easier and more transparent by increasing the coverage of its cadaster and digitizing cadastral plans. Azerbaijan also made property transfer more difficult by making it mandatory to deposit funds into the notary deposit account.

✓ Getting credit
Azerbaijan strengthened access to credit by allowing nonpossessory security interests in one category of movable assets without any restrictions on the use of inventory, including future assets extending automatically to products, proceeds, and replacements of the original collateral. Azerbaijan also allowed the general description of debts and obligations as well as out-of-court enforcement of security interests.

✓ Protecting minority investors
Azerbaijan strengthened minority investor protections by imposing liability on directors for unfair related-party transactions.

× Paying taxes
Azerbaijan made paying taxes more difficult by adding a new labor contribution.

✓ Enforcing contracts
Azerbaijan made enforcing contracts easier by introducing an e-system that allows plaintiffs to file the initial complaint electronically and by adopting a consolidated law on voluntary mediation.

Bahamas, The

✓ Starting a business
The Bahamas made starting a business faster by reducing the registration time for the business license and value added tax and by eliminating the business registration fee.

✓ Getting electricity
The Bahamas made getting electricity more transparent by publishing electricity tariffs online.

× Registering property
The Bahamas made property registration more costly by increasing the stamp duty on property transfers.

✓ Protecting minority investors
The Bahamas strengthened minority investor protections by increasing disclosure requirements for conflicts of interest, clarifying ownership and control structures, and requiring greater corporate transparency.

✓ Paying taxes
The Bahamas made paying taxes easier by enhancing the online value added tax reporting system and making it more accessible to taxpayers.

Bahrain

✓ Dealing with construction permits
Bahrain made obtaining construction permits easier by further streamlining the application process through the new Benayat online platform, and by delegating the application review process to licensed engineering firms.

✓ Getting electricity
Bahrain made the process of getting electricity easier by investing in digitization and transparency of information and by improving its inspection and installation process.

✓ Registering property
Bahrain made property registration easier by streamlining administrative procedures and improving the quality of the land administration system.

✓ Getting credit
Bahrain strengthened access to credit by giving secured creditors absolute priority during insolvency proceedings. During reorganization proceedings, creditors are also now subject to an automatic stay that is limited in time with clear grounds for relief.

✓ Paying taxes
Bahrain made paying taxes easier by implementing electronic payment of social insurance contributions.

✓ Protecting minority investors
Bahrain strengthened minority investor protections by clarifying ownership and control structures.

✓ Trading across borders
Bahrain made exporting faster by deploying new scanners.

✓ **Enforcing contracts**
Bahrain made enforcing contracts easier by creating a specialized commercial court, establishing time standards for key court events, and allowing electronic service of the summons.

✓ **Resolving insolvency**
Bahrain made resolving insolvency easier by introducing a reorganization procedure, allowing debtors to initiate the reorganization procedure, adding provisions on postcommencement financing, and improving voting arrangements.

Bangladesh

✓ **Starting a business**
Bangladesh made starting a business less expensive by reducing name clearance and registration fees and abolishing the fee for certifying digital certificates. This reform applies to both Dhaka and Chittagong.

✓ **Getting electricity**
Bangladesh made getting electricity faster by investing in digitization and human capital at the utility. Bangladesh also made getting electricity less costly by reducing the amount of the security deposit for a new connection. This reform applies to Dhaka.

✓ **Getting credit**
Bangladesh improved access to credit information by expanding the coverage of the credit information bureau.

Barbados

✓ **Getting electricity**
Barbados made getting electricity faster by deploying new software to process applications, increasing the stock of material needed for external connection works, and offering training programs to the utility's engineers.

× **Registering property**
Barbados made transferring property more difficult by increasing the time to record the conveyance at the Land Registry and pay transfer fees and stamp duties.

✓ **Trading across borders**
Barbados made trading across borders easier by streamlining inspections by port authorities and introducing an electronic system for documentary compliance. Barbados made trading across borders more expensive by increasing certificate of origin issuance fees.

✓ **Enforcing contracts**
Barbados made enforcing contracts easier by adopting a law that regulates all aspects of mediation as an alternative dispute resolution mechanism.

Belarus

× Protecting minority investors
Belarus weakened minority investor protections by increasing the time for a joint-stock company to disclose a related-party transaction to the public, the regulator, or the stock exchange.

Belgium

✓ Starting a business
Belgium made starting a business easier by eliminating the paid-in minimum capital requirement.

✓ Paying taxes
Belgium made paying taxes less costly by reducing the corporate income tax rate, increasing the notional interest deduction rate, and decreasing the rates for social security contributions paid by employers.

Belize

✓ Getting electricity
Belize made getting electricity faster by offering training to its utility field engineers and upgrading its geographic information system to map the electricity distribution network.

✓ Trading across borders
Belize made trading across borders easier by enhancing its risk-based management system.

Benin

✓ Registering property
Benin improved the reliability and transparency of the land administration system by publishing official statistics on land transactions and land disputes for the previous calendar year and committing to deliver a legally binding document within a specific time frame.

Brazil

✓ Starting a business
Brazil made starting a business easier by making business registration faster and by decreasing the cost of the digital certificate. This reform applies to both São Paulo and Rio de Janeiro.

✓ Registering property
Brazil made property registration easier by improving the quality of the land administration system. This reform applies to both São Paulo and

Rio de Janeiro. Brazil (São Paulo) also introduced online payment and Brazil (Rio de Janeiro) created an online system to obtain property certificates.

Brunei Darussalam

✓ Enforcing contracts
Brunei Darussalam made enforcing contracts easier by publishing performance measurement reports.

✓ Resolving insolvency
Brunei Darussalam made resolving insolvency easier by increasing the participation of creditors in insolvency proceedings.

Cabo Verde

✓ Starting a business
Cabo Verde made starting a business faster by issuing municipal licenses before conducting an inspection.

✓ Dealing with construction permits
Cabo Verde made dealing with construction permits easier by investing in georeferencing and its geographic information system database.

✓ Getting electricity
Cabo Verde made getting electricity easier by having the utility company obtain municipal excavation permits on behalf of customers, at a reduced cost.

✓ Registering property
Cabo Verde made property registration faster by streamlining administrative procedures and improving the quality of the land administration system.

Cambodia

× Starting a business
Cambodia made starting a business more expensive by increasing the costs associated with business registration at the Ministry of Labor and Vocational Training.

Cameroon

✓ Getting credit
Cameroon improved access to credit information by establishing a framework through the Central African Economic and Monetary Community for the licensing and operation of credit bureaus.

Central African Republic

✓ Getting credit
The Central African Republic improved access to credit information by establishing a framework through the Central African Economic and Monetary Community for the licensing and operation of credit bureaus.

Chad

✓ Registering property
Chad made property registration faster by reducing the time needed to transfer property.

✓ Getting credit
Chad improved access to credit information by establishing a framework through the Central African Economic and Monetary Community for the licensing and operation of credit bureaus.

Chile

✓ Starting a business
Chile made starting a business easier by enabling online registration of closed corporations.

China

✓ Starting a business
China (Beijing) made starting a business easier by fully integrating the obtention of company seals into the one-stop shop.

✓ Dealing with construction permits
China made obtaining building permits easier by simplifying the requirements for low-risk construction projects and by reducing the time to get water and drainage connections. China also made construction safer by imposing stricter qualification requirements for professionals in charge of technical inspections and verifying architectural plans as well as differentiated building quality supervision schemes. This reform applies to both Beijing and Shanghai.

✓ Getting electricity
China made getting electricity easier by streamlining the application process. China also increased the transparency of electricity tariff changes. This reform applies to both Beijing and Shanghai.

✓ Protecting minority investors
China strengthened minority investor protections by imposing liability on controlling shareholders for unfair related-party transactions and clarifying

ownership and control structures. This reform applies to both Beijing and Shanghai.

✓ **Paying taxes**
China made paying taxes easier by implementing a preferential corporate income tax rate for small enterprises, reducing the value added tax rate for certain industries, and enhancing the electronic filing and payment system. This reform applies to both Beijing and Shanghai.

✓ **Trading across borders**
China made exporting and importing easier by implementing advance cargo declaration, upgrading port infrastructure, optimizing customs administration, and publishing fee schedules. This reform applies to both Beijing and Shanghai.

✓ **Enforcing contracts**
China made enforcing contracts easier by regulating the maximum number of adjournments that can be granted and limiting adjournments to unforeseen and exceptional circumstances. This reform applies to both Beijing and Shanghai. China (Shanghai) made enforcing contracts easier by publishing court performance measurement and progress reports.

✓ **Resolving insolvency**
China made resolving insolvency easier by providing rules for post-commencement credit priority and increasing the participation of creditors in insolvency proceedings. This reform applies to both Beijing and Shanghai.

Colombia

✓ **Starting a business**
Colombia made starting a business easier by removing the requirement of opening a bank account to obtain the invoice authorization.

✓ **Trading across borders**
Colombia made trading across borders easier by digitizing the responsibility card, one of its required export documents.

✓ **Resolving insolvency**
Colombia made resolving insolvency easier by increasing the participation of creditors in insolvency proceedings.

Congo, Dem. Rep.

✓ **Starting a business**
The Democratic Republic of Congo made starting a business less expensive by reducing the fees for business incorporation.

✓ Dealing with construction permits

The Democratic Republic of Congo made dealing with construction permits safer by requiring that professionals in charge of plan revisions and inspections be members of the newly created National Order of Architects and National Order of Engineers, and by introducing legislation enforcing inspections during construction.

✓ Paying taxes

The Democratic Republic of Congo made paying taxes less costly by lowering the corporate income tax rate to 30% (from 35%).

Congo, Rep.

✓ Getting credit

The Republic of Congo improved access to credit information by establishing a framework through the Central African Economic and Monetary Community for the licensing and operation of credit bureaus.

Costa Rica

✓ Getting electricity

Costa Rica improved the reliability of electricity supply by repairing the El Porvenir substation, installing 1,140 new poles, and implementing a mapping program for transformers and meters throughout San José. Costa Rica also made getting electricity faster by reducing the time to approve the electrical design.

✓ Enforcing contracts

Costa Rica made enforcing contracts easier by adopting a new code of civil procedure that introduced pretrial conferences as part of the case management techniques in court.

Côte d'Ivoire

✓ Paying taxes

Côte d'Ivoire made paying taxes easier by implementing an electronic filing and payment system, and by introducing an online case management system to process value added tax cash refunds.

✓ Enforcing contracts

Côte d'Ivoire made enforcing contracts easier by publishing reports on commercial court performance and progress of cases.

Croatia

✓ Starting a business
Croatia made starting a business easier by abolishing the requirements to reserve the company name and obtain director signatures for company registration, and by reducing the paid-in minimum capital requirement.

✓ Dealing with construction permits
Croatia made dealing with construction permits less costly by reducing the water contribution for building a warehouse.

✓ Registering property
Croatia made it easier to transfer property by decreasing the real estate transfer tax and by reducing the time to register property title transfers.

× Getting credit
Croatia made accessing credit information more difficult by ending the distribution of individual credit data.

Cyprus

✓ Starting a business
Cyprus made starting a business less expensive by reducing the cost to register a company.

✓ Paying taxes
Cyprus made paying taxes easier by implementing an online system for filing and paying mandatory labor contributions.

Denmark

✓ Dealing with construction permits
Denmark made dealing with construction permits cheaper by eliminating fees for building permits.

Djibouti

✓ Getting credit
Djibouti strengthened access to credit by implementing a functional secured transactions system and a unified notice-based collateral registry.

✓ Protecting minority investors
Djibouti strengthened minority investor protections by increasing corporate transparency.

✓ Resolving insolvency
Djibouti made resolving insolvency easier by facilitating the commencement of proceedings and increasing the effectiveness of court processes.

Employing workers
Djibouti introduced a minimum wage of 35,000 francs ($198) per month.

Dominican Republic

✓ Starting a business
The Dominican Republic made starting a business easier by reducing the minimum capital requirement.

✓ Enforcing contracts
The Dominican Republic made enforcing contracts easier by establishing specialized commercial court divisions and by adopting a framework for mediation and conciliation, including in commercial cases.

Ecuador

✓ Registering property
Ecuador made registering property easier by reducing the time required to transfer property and by increasing the transparency of the land administration system.

Egypt, Arab Rep.

✓ Starting a business
The Arab Republic of Egypt made starting a business easier by abolishing the requirement to obtain a certificate of nonconfusion and improving its one-stop shop.

✓ Getting electricity
Egypt improved the reliability of electricity supply by implementing automated systems to monitor and report power outages.

✓ Protecting minority investors
Egypt strengthened minority investor protections by requiring shareholder approval when listed companies issue new shares.

✓ Paying taxes
Egypt made paying taxes easier by implementing an online system for filing and payment of corporate income tax and value added tax.

El Salvador

✓ Getting electricity

El Salvador made getting electricity easier by accepting electrical plans at the same time as connection requests.

Equatorial Guinea

✓ Starting a business

Equatorial Guinea made starting a business less expensive by reducing registration fees.

✓ Getting credit

Equatorial Guinea improved access to credit information by establishing a framework through the Central African Economic and Monetary Community for the licensing and operation of credit bureaus.

Eswatini

✓ Starting a business

Eswatini made starting a business easier by introducing free online services for name reservation and business registration.

✓ Dealing with construction permits

Eswatini increased the transparency of dealing with construction permits by publishing—online and free of charge—regulations related to construction.

✓ Getting electricity

Eswatini made getting electricity faster by increasing the availability of materials for external connections works.

✓ Registering property

Eswatini improved the quality of its land administration system by publishing the fee schedule, official service standards, and court statistics on land disputes for the previous calendar year. Eswatini also made property registration more expensive by increasing the stamp duty for property transfers.

Ethiopia

✓ Dealing with construction permits

Ethiopia improved building quality control by mandating a final inspection once construction is completed and strengthening qualification requirements for construction professionals.

✓ Registering property
Ethiopia improved the quality of its land administration system by publishing the official list of documents required for property registration as well as statistics on the number of transactions for the previous calendar year and the service standard for delivering a legally binding document.

Finland

✓ Starting a business
Finland made starting a business easier by reducing the fee and processing time of online business registrations.

Gabon

✓ Starting a business
Gabon made starting a business easier by introducing a fast-track business registration process at the one-stop shop.

✓ Dealing with construction permits
Gabon made dealing with construction permits safer by requiring inspections during the construction phase and by appointing a specialized team to conduct final inspections. Gabon also made the process easier by no longer requiring municipal stamps to apply for the permit.

✓ Getting credit
Gabon improved access to credit information by establishing a framework through the Central African Economic and Monetary Community for the licensing and operation of credit bureaus.

Gambia, The

✓ Starting a business
The Gambia made starting a business easier by eliminating the requirement to obtain a company seal.

✓ Paying taxes
The Gambia made paying taxes less costly by decreasing the corporate income tax rate and the turnover tax rate.

Georgia

✓ Dealing with construction permits
Georgia improved its building quality control by increasing public access to information.

Germany

✓ Enforcing contracts

Germany made enforcing contracts easier by introducing electronic filing of the initial complaint and electronic service of process without the need for paper documents.

Ghana

✓ Getting electricity

Ghana made getting electricity faster by improving the review process and increasing the availability of equipment for new electricity connections.

× Paying taxes

Ghana made paying taxes more complicated and more costly by converting a portion of the recoverable value added tax into two new levies that are a cost to the firm: the Ghana Education Trust Fund and the National Health Insurance Levy.

Greece

✓ Starting a business

Greece made starting a business easier by reducing the time to register a company with the commercial registry and removing the requirement to obtain a tax clearance.

✓ Protecting minority investors

Greece strengthened minority investor protections by requiring greater disclosure and an independent review before the approval of related-party transactions as well as greater corporate transparency of executive compensation.

Grenada

✓ Starting a business

Grenada made starting a business easier by introducing online name search.

Guinea

✓ Starting a business

Guinea made starting a business less expensive by reducing the fees for business incorporation.

✓ Registering property
Guinea made property registration less costly by reducing the property transfer registration fee.

× Paying taxes
Guinea made paying taxes more costly by increasing the minimum flat tax (*impôt minimum forfaitaire*) paid by large companies. At the same time, Guinea made paying taxes less costly by reducing the corporate income tax rate and the minimum flat tax rate paid by small and medium-size companies.

Guyana

× Trading across borders
Guyana made trading across borders more expensive by increasing the fees for mandatory inspection through scanners for exports, thereby increasing the cost of export border compliance.

Haiti

✓ Getting credit
Haiti improved access to credit information by expanding the coverage of the credit bureau.

Honduras

✓ Starting a business
Honduras made starting a business less expensive by reducing the notary fees for the preparation of the articles of incorporation.

Hong Kong SAR, China

✓ Dealing with construction permits
Hong Kong SAR, China, made dealing with construction permits easier by enhancing its risk-based approach to inspections.

Hungary

✓ Paying taxes
Hungary made paying taxes easier by upgrading the internal electronic tax system. Hungary also made paying taxes less costly by reducing the social tax rate paid by the employer.

Employing workers
Hungary changed regulations pertaining to overtime work.

India

✓ Starting a business

India made starting a business easier by abolishing filing fees for the SPICe company incorporation form, electronic memorandum of association, and articles of association. This reform applies to both Delhi and Mumbai.

✓ Dealing with construction permits

India (Delhi) streamlined the process, reduced the time and cost of obtaining construction permits, and improved building quality control by strengthening professional certification requirements. India (Mumbai) streamlined the process of obtaining a building permit and made it faster and less expensive to get a construction permit.

✓ Trading across borders

India made trading across borders easier by enabling postclearance audits, integrating trade stakeholders in a single electronic platform, upgrading port infrastructures, and enhancing the electronic submission of documents. This reform applies to both Delhi and Mumbai.

✓ Resolving insolvency

India made resolving insolvency easier by promoting reorganization proceedings in practice. India also made resolving insolvency more difficult by not allowing dissenting creditors to receive as much under reorganization as they would receive in liquidation. This reform applies to both Delhi and Mumbai.

Indonesia

✓ Starting a business

Indonesia (Jakarta) made starting a business easier by introducing an online platform for business licensing and replacing hard copies with electronic certificates.

✓ Getting electricity

Indonesia (Surabaya) improved the reliability of power supply following renovations to and enhanced maintenance of its electrical grid. Indonesia (Surabaya) also made obtaining new electrical connections faster thanks to higher generation capacity.

✓ Paying taxes

Indonesia made paying taxes easier by implementing an online filing and payment system for the major taxes. This reform applies to both Jakarta and Surabaya.

✓ Trading across borders
Indonesia made trading across borders easier by improving the online processing of export customs declarations. This reform applies to both Jakarta and Surabaya.

✓ Enforcing contracts
Indonesia made enforcing contracts easier by introducing an electronic case management system for judges. This reform applies to both Jakarta and Surabaya.

Iran, Islamic Rep.

× Registering property
The Islamic Republic of Iran made transferring property more expensive by increasing the average taxable land value in Tehran City.

Israel

✓ Starting a business
Israel made starting a business easier by allowing joint registration of corporate tax and value added tax.

✓ Getting credit
Israel improved access to credit information by reporting both positive and negative data on individual borrowers.

✓ Paying taxes
Israel made paying taxes easier by implementing an electronic system for filing and paying value added tax and social security contributions. Israel made paying taxes less costly by reducing the corporate income tax rate.

✓ Trading across borders
Israel made exporting easier by eliminating the certificate of origin requirement, thereby decreasing the time and cost of export documentary compliance.

Italy

Employing workers
Italy changed regulations pertaining to fixed-term contracts.

Jamaica

✓ Registering property
Jamaica made property registration easier by reducing the property transfer tax and stamp duty.

✓ Enforcing contracts
Jamaica made enforcing contracts easier by introducing a judicial performance measurement mechanism that provides publicly available information on time to disposition and clearance rate.

Jordan

✓ Getting credit
Jordan strengthened access to credit by introducing a new secured transactions law, amending the insolvency law, and launching a unified, modern, and notice-based collateral registry. The secured transactions law broadened the description of debts and obligations and the scope of assets usable as collateral. The amended insolvency law grants secured creditors absolute priority and provides a time limit and clear grounds for relief from automatic stays during reorganization procedures. Jordan also improved access to credit information by providing credit scores to banks, financial institutions, and borrowers.

✓ Paying taxes
Jordan made paying taxes easier by implementing electronic filing and payment for labor taxes and other mandatory contributions.

✓ Resolving insolvency
Jordan made resolving insolvency easier by introducing a reorganization procedure, by allowing debtors to initiate the reorganization procedure, and by improving the continuation of businesses and the treatment of contracts during insolvency proceedings.

Kazakhstan

✓ Starting a business
Kazakhstan made starting a business easier by registering companies for value added tax at the time of incorporation.

✓ Dealing with construction permits
Kazakhstan made dealing with construction permits easier by streamlining the expert evaluation of the construction project and by improving the process for obtaining a new water connection.

× Registering property
Kazakhstan made registering property cheaper by decreasing registration fees. Kazakhstan also made transferring property more difficult by requiring additional proof of payment of state duties.

✓ Getting credit
Kazakhstan strengthened access to credit by automatically extending security interests to the products, proceeds, and replacements of the original

assets and by giving secured creditors absolute priority during insolvency proceedings. Kazakhstan also improved access to credit information by reporting credit data from retailers.

× Resolving insolvency
Kazakhstan made resolving insolvency more difficult by requiring that all creditors vote on the rehabilitation plan, regardless of its impact on their interests.

Kenya

✓ Dealing with construction permits
Kenya made dealing with construction permits more transparent by making building permit requirements publicly available online, and by reducing fees.

✓ Getting electricity
Kenya improved the reliability of electricity supply by modernizing its existing infrastructure and by inaugurating a new substation in Nairobi.

× Registering property
Kenya made property registration more difficult because of an additional payment slip generation and increased online consent application and title search fees. At the same time, property registration was made faster by moving consents to transfer and payment verification online.

✓ Getting credit
Kenya strengthened access to credit by introducing online registration, modification and cancellation of security interests, and public online searches of its collateral registry.

✓ Protecting minority investors
Kenya strengthened minority investor protections by requiring shareholders to approve the election and dismissal of an external auditor.

✓ Paying taxes
Kenya made paying taxes easier by implementing an online filing and payment system for social security contributions.

✓ Resolving insolvency
Kenya made resolving insolvency easier by improving the continuation of the debtor's business during insolvency proceedings.

Korea, Rep.

✓ Paying taxes
The Republic of Korea made paying taxes easier by introducing additional features to its online filing system for corporate income tax and value added tax.

Kosovo

✓ Dealing with construction permits
Kosovo made dealing with construction permits easier by eliminating the requirement to notify the municipal authority of the start of construction and receive a location inspection.

✓ Getting electricity
Kosovo improved the reliability of power supply by investing in grid infrastructure and by implementing a Supervisory Control and Data Acquisition (SCADA) automatic energy management system for outage monitoring and the restoration of service.

✓ Protecting minority investors
Kosovo strengthened minority investor protections by requiring greater disclosure of transactions with interested parties, extending access to corporate information before trial, clarifying ownership and control structures, and requiring greater corporate transparency.

✓ Enforcing contracts
Kosovo made enforcing contracts easier by introducing a consolidated law on voluntary mediation.

Kuwait

✓ Starting a business
Kuwait made starting a business easier by merging procedures to obtain a commercial license and streamlining online company registration.

✓ Dealing with construction permits
Kuwait made dealing with construction permits easier by streamlining its permitting process, integrating additional authorities to its electronic permitting platform, enhancing interagency communication, and reducing the time to obtain a construction permit.

✓ Getting electricity
Kuwait made getting electricity easier by digitizing the application process, streamlining connection works and meter installations, and using a geographic information system to review connection requests.

✓ Registering property
Kuwait made property registration easier by streamlining the inspection and registration processes. Kuwait also improved the quality of its land administration system by publishing official service standards on property transfers.

✓ Getting credit
Kuwait improved access to credit information by guaranteeing borrowers the legal right to inspect their credit data and offering credit scores as a value-added service to banks and financial institutions.

✓ Protecting minority investors
Kuwait strengthened minority investor protections by providing a 21-day notice for general assembly meetings.

✓ Trading across borders
Kuwait made trading across borders easier by improving the customs risk management system and by implementing a new electronic clearance system.

Kyrgyz Republic

✓ Getting electricity
The Kyrgyz Republic improved the reliability of power supply by enhancing the monitoring of outages and modernizing its infrastructure to reduce power outages.

✓ Getting credit
The Kyrgyz Republic improved access to credit information by providing credit scores to banks, financial institutions, and borrowers.

✓ Paying taxes
The Kyrgyz Republic made paying taxes easier by consolidating the tax on interest income into the corporate income tax and by implementing an online platform for filing and paying taxes.

Lao PDR

✓ Starting a business
The Lao People's Democratic Republic made starting a business easier by eliminating the requirement to obtain proof of business location from the Village Chief Authority for business registration.

✓ Getting electricity
Lao PDR made getting electricity faster by allocating more staff to process applications. Lao PDR also improved the reliability of power supply by deploying an automated Supervisory Control and Data Acquisition (SCADA) system for outage monitoring and the restoration of service.

Latvia

× Paying taxes
Latvia made paying taxes costlier by increasing the effective corporate income tax burden. The new calculations replaced the corporate income tax paid on the taxable profits of companies with an income tax based on distributed profits.

Lebanon

✓ Enforcing contracts
Lebanon made enforcing contracts easier by adopting a law that regulates all aspects of mediation as an alternative dispute resolution mechanism.

Lesotho

✓ Starting a business
Lesotho made starting a business easier by removing the requirement for a health certificate and the inspection of the premises for all businesses.

Liberia

× Paying taxes
Liberia made paying taxes more costly by increasing the employer-paid social security contribution rate.

× Trading across borders
Liberia made trading across borders more expensive by requiring traders to obtain Cargo Tracking Note certificates, thereby increasing the cost of documentary compliance for exports and imports.

Lithuania

✓ Getting electricity
Lithuania made getting electricity easier by launching an integrated digital application and by reducing the cost of new connections.

✓ Protecting minority investors
Lithuania strengthened minority investor protections by clarifying ownership and control structures.

Luxembourg

Employing workers
Luxembourg changed regulations pertaining to paid annual leave.

Madagascar

✓ Enforcing contracts
Madagascar made enforcing contracts easier by publishing performance measurement and progress reports for the commercial court.

Malaysia

✓ Dealing with construction permits
Malaysia streamlined the process of dealing with construction permits by eliminating the road and drainage inspection performed by Kuala Lumpur City Hall.

Mali

× Paying taxes
Mali made paying taxes more difficult by introducing a new tax, the solidarity contribution, which is levied at a rate of 0.5% on the business turnover.

Malta

✓ Starting a business
Malta made starting a business easier by implementing an online one-stop shop for the registration of employers, employees, and value added tax.

✓ Getting electricity
Malta increased the reliability of power supply by upgrading its power grid infrastructure and launching a network planning and operations control center.

Employing workers
Malta changed regulations pertaining to paid annual leave.

Mauritania

✓ Getting credit
Mauritania improved access to credit information by launching a new credit reporting system, distributing both positive and negative data, and offering credit scores to banks and financial institutions.

✓ Enforcing contracts
Mauritania made enforcing contracts easier by introducing a simplified procedure for small claims, setting time standards for key court events, and limiting adjournments. Mauritania also adopted a law that regulates all aspects of mediation as an alternative dispute resolution mechanism.

Mauritius

✓ Dealing with construction permits
Mauritius streamlined the process of dealing with construction permits by simplifying the process of plan approvals from utilities and reducing the time to apply for wastewater connection.

✓ Registering property
Mauritius made property registration faster by making it easier to check for encumbrances. Mauritius also improved the quality of its land administration system by publishing official service standards and court statistics on land disputes.

✓ Enforcing contracts
Mauritius made enforcing contracts easier by publishing performance measurement reports for the commercial division of the Supreme Court.

✓ Resolving insolvency
Mauritius made resolving insolvency easier by improving the continuation of the debtor's business during insolvency proceedings.

Mexico

× Dealing with construction permits
Mexico (Mexico City) made dealing with construction permits more difficult by increasing the fees for obtaining a building permit.

Moldova

✓ Dealing with construction permits
Moldova made dealing with construction permits easier by enabling quality control by supervising engineers and by no longer requiring clearances from health and environmental agencies for low-risk structures.

✓ Paying taxes
Moldova made paying taxes easier by reducing the social security contribution rate paid by the employer and the capital gains basis. At the same time, the value of the environmental tax and the time for labor taxes and contributions increased.

✓ Enforcing contracts
Moldova made enforcing contracts easier by amending the code of civil procedure to establish a simplified procedure for small claims.

Morocco

✓ Dealing with construction permits
Morocco made dealing with construction permits easier by improving its online platform and further streamlining the process, making it possible to apply for and obtain certificates of conformity online.

✓ Getting electricity
Morocco made getting electricity easier by generalizing online applications for new connections and expanding the use of prebuilt transformers.

× **Registering property**
Morocco made property registration less transparent by not publishing statistics on the number of property transactions and land disputes for the previous calendar year. Morocco also made property registration faster by reducing the time to obtain a nonencumbrance certificate.

✓ **Protecting minority investors**
Morocco strengthened minority investor protections by expanding shareholders' role in major transactions, promoting independent directors, increasing transparency on directors' employment in other companies, and making it easier to request general meetings.

✓ **Paying taxes**
Morocco made paying taxes less costly by reducing the corporate income tax rate.

✓ **Trading across borders**
Morocco made trading across borders faster by introducing e-payment of port fees, streamlining paperless customs clearance, and extending port hours of operation.

✓ **Enforcing contracts**
Morocco made enforcing contracts easier by introducing an automated system that randomly assigns cases to judges and by publishing court measurement performance reports.

Myanmar

✓ **Starting a business**
Myanmar made starting a business easier by introducing an online platform for company registration and by reducing incorporation fees.

✓ **Dealing with construction permits**
Myanmar strengthened construction quality control by imposing stricter qualification requirements for architects and engineers and making building permitting requirements available online. Myanmar also improved its water and sanitation infrastructure and made the building permitting process more efficient by introducing service quality standards.

✓ **Registering property**
Myanmar made property registration faster by streamlining deed registration and appraisal. Myanmar also improved the quality of its land administration system by publishing the fee schedule, official service standards, and statistics on property transfers for the previous calendar year.

✓ **Protecting minority investors**
Myanmar strengthened minority investor protections by requiring greater disclosure of transactions with interested parties, increasing director liability, and requiring greater corporate transparency.

✓ **Enforcing contracts**
Myanmar made enforcing contracts easier by publishing performance measurement reports.

Nepal

× **Starting a business**
Nepal made starting a business more difficult by requiring in-person follow-up for employee registration for social security.

✓ **Dealing with construction permits**
Nepal made dealing with construction permits easier and less costly by reducing fees for building permits and improving the online e-submissions platform.

× **Registering property**
Nepal made property registration more expensive by increasing the property transfer registration fee. Nepal also improved the quality of its land administration system by publishing official service standards for delivering updated cadastral maps.

✓ **Getting credit**
Nepal improved access to credit information by expanding the coverage of the credit bureau.

✓ **Trading across borders**
Nepal reduced the time and cost to export and the time to import by opening the Integrated Check Post Birgunj at the Nepal–India border.

✓ **Enforcing contracts**
Nepal made enforcing contracts easier by adopting a new code of civil procedure that introduces time standards for key court events.

Niger

✓ **Getting credit**
Niger improved access to credit information by expanding the coverage of the credit bureau and beginning to distribute data from utility companies.

Nigeria

✓ **Starting a business**
Nigeria made starting a business easier by reducing the time needed to register a company and by improving online platforms. This reform applies to both Kano and Lagos. Nigeria (Kano) also made starting a business easier by no longer requiring on-site inspections for business premises registration.

✓ **Dealing with construction permits**
Nigeria (Lagos) made dealing with construction permits less costly by eliminating the Infrastructure Development Charge (IDC, the fee for construction permits) for warehouses.

✓ **Getting electricity**
Nigeria made getting electricity easier by allowing certified engineers to conduct inspections for new connections. This reform applies to both Kano and Lagos.

✓ **Registering property**
Nigeria (Lagos) improved its land administration system by implementing a geographic information system.

✓ **Trading across borders**
Nigeria reduced the time to export and import by further upgrading its electronic system and by launching e-payment of fees. This reform applies to both Kano and Lagos.

✓ **Enforcing contracts**
Nigeria made enforcing contracts easier by introducing a pretrial conference as part of the case management techniques used in court. This reform applies to both Kano and Lagos. Nigeria (Kano) also made enforcing contracts easier by issuing new rules of civil procedure for small claims courts, which limit adjournments to unforeseen and exceptional circumstances.

North Macedonia

✓ **Enforcing contracts**
North Macedonia made enforcing contracts easier by simplifying the calculation of enforcement fees as well as making the overall process less costly.

Employing workers
North Macedonia changed its labor regulations on probationary period, priority rules during redundancy dismissals and reemployment, and severance payments.

Oman

✓ **Getting electricity**
Oman made getting electricity faster by investing in prepaid meters and enforcing service delivery time frames.

✓ **Registering property**
Oman made registering property faster by reducing the time to issue deeds and improved its land administration system by publishing official service standards on property transfers.

✓ **Protecting minority investors**
Oman strengthened minority investor protections by increasing shareholder rights as well as clarifying ownership and control structures.

✓ **Trading across borders**
Oman made importing and exporting faster by upgrading infrastructure at the Sohar Port as well as introducing risk-based inspections and postclearance audits.

Pakistan

✓ **Starting a business**
Pakistan made starting a business easier by expanding procedures available through the online one-stop shop. This reform applies to both Karachi and Lahore. Furthermore, Pakistan (Lahore) abolished the Labor Department registration fee.

✓ **Dealing with construction permits**
Pakistan (Karachi) made obtaining a construction permit easier and faster by streamlining the approval process and also made construction safer by ensuring that building quality inspections take place regularly. Pakistan (Lahore) also made obtaining a construction permit easier and faster by streamlining the approval process and by improving the operational efficiency of its one-stop shop for construction permitting.

✓ **Getting electricity**
Pakistan made getting electricity easier by enforcing service delivery time frames and by launching an online portal for new applications. Pakistan also increased the transparency of electricity tariff changes. This reform applies to both Karachi and Lahore.

✓ **Registering property**
Pakistan (Karachi) made property registration faster by making it easier to execute and register a deed at the Office of the Sub-Registrar. Pakistan (Lahore) made registering property easier by increasing the transparency of the land administration system.

✓ **Paying taxes**
Pakistan made paying taxes easier by introducing online payment modules for value added tax and corporate income tax, and less costly by reducing the corporate income tax rate. This reform applies to both Karachi and Lahore.

✓ **Trading across borders**
Pakistan made trading across borders easier by enhancing the integration of various agencies in the Web-Based One Customs (WEBOC) electronic system and coordinating joint physical inspections at the port. This reform applies to both Karachi and Lahore.

Papua New Guinea

✓ Paying taxes

Papua New Guinea made paying taxes less costly by abolishing the training levy. Papua New Guinea made paying taxes easier by issuing value added tax refunds more quickly thanks to more streamlined audits.

✓ Trading across borders

Papua New Guinea made trading across borders easier by implementing an automated customs data management system. At the same time, Papua New Guinea made trading across borders more expensive by increasing port fees.

Paraguay

✓ Enforcing contracts

Paraguay made enforcing contracts easier by introducing an electronic case management system for judges and lawyers.

Peru

✓ Trading across borders

Peru reduced the time to export and import by introducing electronic mandates for customs brokers and by streamlining import customs clearances.

Philippines

✓ Starting a business

The Philippines made starting a business easier by abolishing the minimum capital requirement for domestic companies.

✓ Dealing with construction permits

The Philippines made dealing with construction permits easier by improving coordination and streamlining the process for obtaining an occupancy certificate.

✓ Protecting minority investors

The Philippines strengthened minority investor protections by requiring greater disclosure of transactions with interested parties and enhancing director liability for transactions with interested parties.

Poland

✓ Getting electricity

Poland made getting electricity faster by implementing a new customer service platform that allows the utility to better track applications for new commercial connections.

× Registering property
Poland made transferring property more difficult by increasing the time needed to apply for registration at the Land and Mortgage Registry.

Qatar

✓ Getting electricity
Qatar made getting electricity faster by reducing the time for processing online applications for a new connection.

✓ Registering property
Qatar made property registration easier by streamlining property registration procedures. Qatar also improved the quality of its land administration system by publishing official service standards on property transfers and court statistics on land disputes for the previous calendar year.

✓ Getting credit
Qatar improved access to credit information by reporting credit data from a telecommunications company.

Romania

✓ Starting a business
Romania made starting a business easier by allowing voluntary value added tax registration, which is less time consuming than mandatory registration.

✓ Paying taxes
Romania made paying taxes less costly by eliminating five employer-paid taxes and contributions. At the same time, Romania introduced a new work insurance contribution paid by the employer.

Russian Federation

✓ Getting electricity
The Russian Federation made getting electricity faster by setting new deadlines and establishing specialized departments for connection works within the utilities of Moscow and St. Petersburg.

✓ Protecting minority investors
Russia strengthened minority investor protections by requiring greater corporate transparency. This reform applies to both Moscow and St. Petersburg.

✓ Paying taxes
Russia made paying taxes easier by reducing the tax authority review period of taxpayer applications for value added tax cash refunds and by further enhancing the 1C software used for tax and payroll preparation. This reform applies to both Moscow and St. Petersburg.

Rwanda

✓ Starting a business
Rwanda made starting a business easier by exempting newly formed small and medium-size enterprises from paying the trading license tax for their first two years of operation.

✓ Dealing with construction permits
Rwanda made dealing with construction permits faster by reducing the time to obtain a water and sewage connection. Rwanda also improved building quality control by requiring all construction professionals to obtain liability insurance on buildings once in use.

✓ Getting electricity
Rwanda improved the reliability of power supply by upgrading its power grid infrastructure.

Employing workers
Rwanda changed regulations pertaining to weekly rest, working hours, severance payments, and reemployment priority rules after redundancy dismissals.

San Marino

✓ Starting a business
San Marino made starting a business easier by extending the deadline to deposit the paid-in capital.

Saudi Arabia

✓ Starting a business
Saudi Arabia made starting a business easier by establishing a one-stop shop that merged several pre- and postregistration procedures. Saudi Arabia also eliminated the requirement for married women to provide additional documents when applying for a national identity card.

✓ Dealing with construction permits
Saudi Arabia made dealing with construction permits easier by launching an online platform and by enabling civil defense approval after the issuance of the building permit.

✓ Getting electricity
Saudi Arabia made getting electricity easier by streamlining connection works and meter installation, by using a geographic information system to review new electrical connection requests, and by no longer requiring certificates of completion.

✓ Getting credit
Saudi Arabia strengthened access to credit by introducing a secured transactions law and an insolvency law. The new laws provide secured creditors with absolute priority inside bankruptcy, allow all types of debts and obligations to be secured between the parties, and allow out-of-court enforcement of security interests.

✓ Protecting minority investors
Saudi Arabia strengthened minority investor protections by increasing access to evidence at trial.

Paying taxes
Saudi Arabia introduced a value added tax.

✓ Trading across borders
Saudi Arabia made importing and exporting easier by enhancing its electronic trade single window, enabling risk-based inspections, launching an online platform for certification of imported goods, and upgrading infrastructure at the Jeddah Port.

✓ Enforcing contracts
Saudi Arabia made enforcing contracts easier by publishing court performance measurement reports and information on the progress of cases through the court.

✓ Resolving insolvency
Saudi Arabia made resolving insolvency easier by introducing a reorganization procedure, allowing debtors to initiate the reorganization procedure, improving voting arrangements in reorganization, improving the continuation of businesses and the treatment of contracts during insolvency proceedings, allowing postcommencement credit, and increasing the participation of creditors in the insolvency proceedings.

Senegal

✓ Getting credit
Senegal improved access to credit information by expanding the coverage of the credit bureau and offering credit scoring as a value-added service.

✓ Paying taxes
Senegal made paying taxes easier by implementing an electronic filing and payment system and less costly by merging several taxes.

Serbia

× Starting a business
Serbia made starting a business more complicated by requiring that entrepreneurs obtain an electronic certificate and register the ultimate beneficial owners separately after incorporation.

✓ **Dealing with construction permits**
Serbia made dealing with construction permits easier by implementing a new online portal and by reducing administrative fees.

✓ **Getting electricity**
Serbia improved the reliability of power supply by reengineering substations, installing remote control systems, and improving grid maintenance.

✓ **Protecting minority investors**
Serbia strengthened minority investor protections by requiring an external review and immediate disclosure of related-party transactions, clarifying ownership and control structures as well as requiring greater corporate transparency.

✓ **Paying taxes**
Serbia made paying taxes easier by introducing internal deadlines to refund value added tax credits.

✓ **Enforcing contracts**
Serbia made enforcing contracts easier by establishing financial incentives for the parties to attempt mediation.

✓ **Resolving insolvency**
Serbia made resolving insolvency easier by requiring creditors to approve the appointment of the insolvency representative and providing them with the right to information on the financial status of the debtor.

Seychelles

✓ **Dealing with construction permits**
The Seychelles made dealing with construction permits faster by streamlining internal processes.

Sierra Leone

✓ **Trading across borders**
Sierra Leone made trading across borders faster by upgrading its customs electronic data interchange system, thereby reducing the time for import documentary compliance.

Singapore

✓ **Dealing with construction permits**
Singapore made dealing with construction permits easier by enhancing its risk-based approach to inspections, improving public access to soil information, and streamlining the process to obtain a construction permit.

Slovak Republic

✓ Starting a business
The Slovak Republic made starting a business easier by abolishing the requirement to obtain and submit information on tax arrears.

Employing workers
The Slovak Republic increased wage premiums for work performed during days of weekly rest and at night.

South Africa

✓ Enforcing contracts
South Africa made enforcing contracts easier by introducing a specialized court dedicated to hearing commercial cases.

Employing workers
South Africa introduced a national minimum wage.

Spain

✓ Protecting minority investors
Spain strengthened minority investor protections by clarifying ownership and control structures.

St. Kitts and Nevis

✓ Getting credit
St. Kitts and Nevis improved access to credit information through the introduction of regulations that govern the licensing and functioning of credit bureaus in the member states of the East Caribbean Currency Union (ECCU).

St. Vincent and the Grenadines

✓ Paying taxes
St. Vincent and the Grenadines made paying taxes less costly by reducing the corporate income tax rate.

Sudan

× Getting electricity
Sudan decreased the reliability of power supply by not collecting and reporting data on the frequency and duration of power outages as measured by the system average interruption duration index (SAIDI) and system average interruption frequency index (SAIFI) indexes.

× Getting credit
Sudan weakened access to credit by removing provisions that grant priority to secured creditors' claims inside bankruptcy procedures and provide for reorganization procedures.

× Resolving insolvency
Sudan made resolving insolvency more difficult by worsening the treatment of contracts during insolvency proceedings and weakening creditors' rights.

Suriname

Employing workers
Suriname changed regulations pertaining to fixed-term contracts.

Taiwan, China

× Paying taxes
Taiwan, China, made paying taxes costlier by increasing the corporate income tax rate.

Tajikistan

✓ Starting a business
Tajikistan made starting a business easier by registering companies for a Social Identification Number at the time of incorporation.

✓ Getting credit
Tajikistan strengthened access to credit by launching a unified, modern, and notice-based collateral registry; introducing a functional secured transactions system; broadening the scope of assets that can be used as collateral; allowing the general description of debts and obligations; granting secured creditors absolute priority; and providing a time limit and clear grounds for relief from automatic stays during reorganization procedures.

✓ Trading across borders
Tajikistan made exporting faster by prioritizing customs clearance of perishable goods exports.

Thailand

✓ Dealing with construction permits
Thailand made dealing with construction permits easier by introducing legislation requiring phased inspections during construction.

Timor-Leste

× Paying taxes
Timor-Leste made paying taxes costlier by introducing a social security contribution scheme paid by the employer.

Togo

✓ Starting a business
Togo made starting a business easier by abolishing the requirement to notarize company documents and by reducing the time to register a company.

✓ Dealing with construction permits
Togo made dealing with construction permits easier by reducing fees and by adopting an online portal for the submission of applications. Togo made dealing with construction permits more transparent by making the required documents, preapproval, and fees available online. Togo also improved its building quality control by regulating inspections during construction.

✓ Getting electricity
Togo made getting electricity less costly by further reducing the cost of connection works and the security deposit for new connections.

✓ Registering property
Togo made property registration easier by streamlining administrative procedures and reducing costs.

✓ Getting credit
Togo improved access to credit information by expanding the coverage of the credit bureau and beginning to distribute data from utility companies.

Tonga

× Dealing with construction permits
Tonga made dealing with construction permits less transparent by removing online public information on the building code, building fees, and required preapprovals.

Trinidad and Tobago

✓ Paying taxes
Trinidad and Tobago made paying taxes easier by conducting limited scope audits instead of full audits for value added tax refunds.

Tunisia

✓ Starting a business
Tunisia made starting a business easier by merging more services into the one-stop shop and reducing fees.

✓ Registering property
Tunisia made property registration faster by streamlining the internal process to transfer property. Tunisia also increased the transparency of the land administration by publishing statistics tracking property transactions at the Land Registry.

✓ Paying taxes
Tunisia made paying taxes easier by implementing a risk-based tax audit system.

Turkey

✓ Registering property
Turkey made property registration less expensive by temporarily reducing mortar charges to transfer property, and faster by reducing the time to obtain a tax assessment.

✓ Paying taxes
Turkey made paying taxes easier by amending the value added tax code to exempt certain capital investments from value added tax.

Uganda

✓ Getting electricity
Uganda improved the monitoring and regulation of power outages by improving its calculations of the annual system average interruption duration index (SAIDI) and system average interruption frequency index (SAIFI).

Ukraine

✓ Dealing with construction permits
Ukraine streamlined the dealing with construction permits process by eliminating the requirement to hire an external supervisor and introducing an online notification system. Ukraine also made obtaining a construction permit less costly by reducing the contribution fee to the Kyiv City Council.

✓ Getting electricity
Ukraine made getting electricity easier by streamlining the issuance of technical conditions and by implementing a geographic information system. Ukraine also improved the reliability of power supply by introducing an outage compensation mechanism.

✓ Registering property
Ukraine made registering property easier by increasing the transparency of the land administration system.

✓ Getting credit
Ukraine improved access to credit information by establishing a new public credit registry in the National Bank of Ukraine.

✓ Protecting minority investors
Ukraine strengthened minority investor protections by requiring greater disclosure of transactions with interested parties.

✓ Trading across borders
Ukraine reduced the time to import by simplifying conformity certification requirements for auto parts.

United Arab Emirates

✓ Starting a business
The United Arab Emirates made starting a business less expensive by reducing the fees for business incorporation.

✓ Dealing with construction permits
The United Arab Emirates made dealing with construction permits easier by using a risk-based approach to reduce the number of inspections.

✓ Protecting minority investors
The United Arab Emirates increased minority investor protections by providing for disqualification of directors in cases of prejudicial conflicts of interest.

Paying taxes
The United Arab Emirates introduced a value added tax.

✓ Trading across borders
The United Arab Emirates made trading across borders easier by reducing the time to export by fully digitizing certificates of origin and the cost to import by issuing certificates of conformity that cover multiple shipments.

United Kingdom

× Paying taxes
The United Kingdom made paying taxes more difficult by introducing a new pension scheme paid by the employer.

United States

✓ Starting a business

The United States (Los Angeles) made starting a business easier by introducing online filing of the statement of information for limited liability companies.

✓ Paying taxes

The United States made paying taxes less costly by decreasing the corporate income tax rate. This reform applies to both New York City and Los Angeles.

✓ Enforcing contracts

The United States (Los Angeles) made enforcing contracts easier by introducing electronic filing and electronic payment of court fees.

Uruguay

✓ Trading across borders

Uruguay reduced the time required for import documentary compliance by introducing electronic certificates of origin.

Uzbekistan

✓ Protecting minority investors

Uzbekistan strengthened minority investor protections by increasing shareholders' rights and role in major corporate decisions, clarifying ownership and control structures, and requiring greater corporate transparency.

✓ Paying taxes

Uzbekistan made paying taxes easier by merging the infrastructure tax with the corporate income tax.

✓ Trading across borders

Uzbekistan made trading across borders easier by introducing risk-based inspections and simplifying import documentary compliance.

✓ Enforcing contracts

Uzbekistan made enforcing contracts easier by introducing a consolidated law on voluntary mediation, establishing financial incentives for the parties to attempt mediation, and publishing performance measurement reports on local commercial courts.

Vietnam

✓ Getting credit

Vietnam improved access to credit information by distributing data from retailers.

✓ Paying taxes
Vietnam made paying taxes easier by upgrading the information technology infrastructure used by the General Department of Taxation.

Zambia

✓ Protecting minority investors
Zambia strengthened minority investor protections by increasing shareholders' rights and role in major corporate decisions as well as clarifying ownership and control structures.

✓ Resolving insolvency
Zambia made resolving insolvency easier by introducing a reorganization procedure and granting debtors the possibility of obtaining postcommencement finance.

Zimbabwe

✓ Starting a business
Zimbabwe made starting a business easier by improving online name search and by reducing the Harare Municipality business licensing fee.

✓ Dealing with construction permits
Zimbabwe made dealing with construction permits faster by streamlining plan approvals.

✓ Registering property
Zimbabwe made property registration easier by reducing the time to transfer property and increased transparency by publishing official statistics on land disputes for the previous calendar year.

✓ Getting credit
Zimbabwe strengthened access to credit by giving secured creditors absolute priority during insolvency proceedings.

✓ Resolving insolvency
Zimbabwe made resolving insolvency easier by introducing a new reorganization procedure, allowing creditors to vote on the reorganization plan, and granting debtors the possibility of obtaining postcommencement finance.

CHAPTER 8

References

Acharya, Viral V., Ramin P. Baghai, and Krishnamurthy V. Subramanian. 2013. "Labor Laws and Innovation." *Journal of Law and Economics* 56 (4): 997–99.

Ades, A., and R. Di Tella. 1997. "National Champions and Corruption: Some Unpleasant Interventionist Arithmetic." *Economic Journal* 107: 1023–42.

Ahn, JaeBin, Zidong An, John Bluedorn, Gabriele Ciminelli, Zsóka Kóczán, Davide Malacrino, Daniela Muhaj, and Patricia Neidlinger. 2019. "Work in Progress: Improving Youth Labor Market Outcomes in Emerging Market and Developing Economies." IMF Staff Discussion Note 19/02, International Monetary Fund, Washington, DC.

Ahsan, Reshad N. 2013. "Input Tariffs, Speed of Contract Enforcement, and the Productivity of Firms in India." *Journal of International Economics* 90 (1): 181–92.

Alfaro, Laura, and Anusha Chari. 2014. "Deregulation, Misallocation, and Size: Evidence from India." *Journal of Law and Economics* 57 (4): 897–936.

Alimov, Azizjon. 2015. "Labor Protection Laws and Bank Loan Contracting." *Journal of Law and Economics* 58 (1): 37–74.

Allcott, Hunt, Allan Collard-Wexler, and Stephen D. O'Connell. 2016. "How Do Electricity Shortages Affect Industry? Evidence from India." *American Economic Review* 106 (3): 587–624.

Almeida, Rita, and Pedro Manuel Carneiro. 2009. "Enforcement of Labor Regulation and Firm Size." *Journal of Comparative Economics* 37 (1): 28–46.

Alvarez, Roberto, and Rodrigo Fuentes. 2018. "Minimum Wage and Productivity: Evidence from Chilean Manufacturing Plants." *Economic Development and Cultural Change* 67 (1): 193–224.

Amirapu, Amrit, and Michael Gechter. 2019. "Labor Regulations and the Cost of Corruption: Evidence from the Indian Firm Size Distribution." *Review of Economics and Statistics*, June 4.

Andersen, Thomas Barnebeck, and Carl-Johan Dalgaard. 2013. "Power Outages and Economic Growth in Africa." *Energy Economics* 38 (July): 19–23.

Asmal, Zaakhir, Haroon Bhorat, Ravi Kanbur, Marco Ranzani, and Pierella Paci. 2018. "Minimum Wages and Labor Supply in an Emerging Market." Policy Research Working Paper 8681, World Bank, Washington, DC.

Asturias, Jose, Sewon Hur, Timothy J. Kehoe, and Kim Ruhl. 2017. "Firm Entry and Exit and Aggregate Growth." NBER Working Paper 23202, National Bureau of Economic Research, Cambridge, MA.

Auriol, Emmanuelle. 2006. "Corruption in Procurement and Public Purchase." *International Journal of Industrial Organization* 24 (5): 867–85.

Awasthi, Rajul, and Nihal Bayraktar. 2015. "Can Tax Simplification Help Lower Tax Corruption?" *Eurasian Economic Review* (5) 2: 297–330.

Bardhan, P. 1997. "Corruption and Development: A Review of Issues." *Journal of Economic Literature* 35: 1320–46.

Beck, Thorsten, Chen Lin, and Yue Ma. 2014. "Why Do Firms Evade Taxes? The Role of Information Sharing and Financial Sector Outreach." *Journal of Finance* 69 (2): 763–817.

Belitski, Maksim, Farzana Chowdhury, and Sameeksha Desai. 2016. "Taxes, Corruption and Entry." *Small Business Economics* 47 (1): 201–16.

Benhassine, Najy, David McKenzie, Victor Pouliquen, and Massimiliano Santini. 2018. "Does Inducing Informal Firms to Formalize Make Sense? Experimental Evidence from Benin." *Journal of Public Economics* 157 (January): 1–14.

Berkowitz, Daniel, Chen Lin, and Yue Ma. 2015. "Do Property Rights Matter? Evidence from a Property Law Enactment." *Journal of Financial Economics* 116 (3): 583–93.

Bertók, J. 2005. "The Role of Transparency in Preventing Corruption in Public Procurement: Issues for Consideration." In *Fighting Corruption and Promoting Integrity in Public Procurement*, edited by Organisation for Economic Cooperation and Development (OECD), 45–50. Paris: OECD Publishing.

Betcherman, Gordon, N. Meltem Daysal, and Carmen Pagés. 2010. "Do Employment Subsidies Work? Evidence from Regionally Targeted Subsidies in Turkey." *Labour Economics* 17 (4): 710–22.

Bjuggren, Carl Magnus. 2018. "Employment Protection and Labor Productivity." *Journal of Public Economics* 157 (January): 138–57.

Botero, Juan Carlos, Simeon Djankov, Rafael La Porta, Florencio López-de-Silanes, and Andrei Shleifer. 2004. "The Regulation of Labor." *Quarterly Journal of Economics* 119 (4): 1339–82.

Bottasso, Anna, Maurizio Conti, and Giovanni Sulis. 2016. "Firm Dynamics and Employment Protection: Evidence from Sectoral Data." Discussion Paper 9740, Institute of Labor Economics IZA, Bonn.

Braunerhjelm, Pontus, and Johan Eklund. 2014. "Taxes, Tax Administrative Burdens and New Firm Formation." *Kyklos* 67 (1): 1–11.

Brown, James R., Gustav Martinsson, and Bruce C. Petersen. 2013. "Law, Stock Markets, and Innovation." *The Journal of the American Finance Association* 68 (4): 1517–49.

Calomiris, Charles, Mauricio Larrain, José Liberti, and Jason Sturgess. 2017. "How Collateral Laws Shape Lending and Sectoral Activity." *Journal of Financial Economics* 123 (1): 163–88.

Campos, J. Edgardo, and Sanjay Pradhan, eds. 2007. *The Many Faces of Corruption: Tracking Vulnerabilities at the Sector Level*. Washington, DC: World Bank.

Chakraborty, Pavel. 2016. "Judicial Quality and Regional Firm Performance: The Case of Indian States." *Journal of Comparative Economics* 44 (4): 902–18.

Che Azmi, Anna A., and Yusniza Kamarulzaman. 2009. "Adoption of Tax E-filing: A Conceptual Paper." *African Journal of Business Management* 4 (5): 599–603.

Chemin, Matthieu. 2018. "Judicial Efficiency and Firm Productivity: Evidence from a World Database of Judicial Reforms." *Review of Economics and Statistics*, November 2.

Chidolue, C. A., A. I. Nwajuaku, and V. O. Okonkwo. 2013. "Rehabilitation of Onitsha-Enugu Dual Carriageway in Anambra State, Nigeria: Lessons Learned." *Nigerian Journal of Technology (NIJOTECH)* 32 (3): 393–402.

Chong, Uven, and Omar Hopkins. 2016. "An International Experience on the Evolution of Road Costs during the Project Life Cycle." *Transport Policy* 48: 60–66.

Choi, Jieun, Mark Dutz, and Zainab Usman. 2019. *The Future of Work in Africa: Harnessing the Potential of Digital Technologies for All*. World Bank: Washington, DC.

Claessens, Stijn, Kenichi Ueda, and Yishay Yafeh. 2014. "Institutions and Financial Frictions: Estimating with Structural Restrictions on Firm Value and Investment." *Journal of Development Economics* 110 (September): 107–22.

Cockx, Bart, and Matteo Picchio. 2012. "Are Short-Lived Jobs Stepping Stones to Long-Lasting Jobs?" *Oxford Bulletin of Economics and Statistics* 74 (5): 646–75.

Cole, Matthew A., Robert J.R. Elliott, Giovanni Occhiali, and Eric Strobl. 2018. "Power Outages and Firm Performance in Sub-Saharan Africa." *Journal of Development Economics* 134 (September): 150–59.

Collewet, Marion, and Jan Sauerman. 2017. "Working Hours and Productivity." Discussion Paper 10722, Institute of Labor Economics IZA, Bonn.

Collier, Paul, Martina Kirchberger, and Måns Söderbom. 2015. "The Cost of Road Infrastructure in Low and Middle Income Countries." Policy Research Working Paper 7408, World Bank, Washington, DC.

Corcoran, Adrian, and Robert Gillanders. 2015. "Foreign Direct Investment and the Ease of Doing Business." *Review of World Economics* 151 (1): 103–26.

Cournède, B., O. Denk, and P. Garda. 2016. "Effects of Flexibility-Enhancing Reforms on Employment Transitions." OECD Economics Department Working Papers 1348, OECD Publishing, Paris.

Coviello, Decio, and Mario Mariniello. 2014. "Publicity Requirements in Public Procurement: Evidence from a Regression Discontinuity Design." *Journal of Public Economics* 109 (January): 76–100.

Cremers, Martijn, and Allen Ferrell. 2014. "Thirty Years of Shareholder Rights and Firm Valuation." *Journal of Finance* 69 (3): 1167–96.

Decarolis, Francesco, and Giuliana Palumbo. 2015. "Renegotiation of Public Contracts: An Empirical Analysis." *Economics Letters* 132 (July): 77–81.

Demenet, Axel, Mireille Razafindrakoto, and François Roubaud. 2016. "Do Informal Businesses Gain from Registration and How? Panel Data Evidence from Vietnam." *World Development* 84 (August): 326–41.

Dermigüç-Kunt, Asli, Bálint L. Horváth, and Harry Huizinga. 2017. "How Does Long Term Finance Affect Economic Volatility?" *Journal of Financial Stability* 33 (December): 41–59.

Dierkes, Maik, Carsten Erner, Thomas Langer, and Lars Norden. 2013. "Business Credit Information Sharing and Default Risk of Private Firms." *Journal of Banking & Finance* 37 (8): 2867–78.

Di Tella, Rafael, and Robert MacCulloch. 2005. "The Consequence of Labor Market Flexibility: Panel Evidence Based on Survey Data." *European Economic Review* 49 (5): 1225–59.

Djankov, Simeon. 2016. "The Doing Business Project: How It Started: Correspondence." *Journal of Economic Perspectives* 30 (1): 247–48.

Djankov, Simeon, and Rita Ramalho. 2009. "Employment Laws in Developing Countries." *Journal of Comparative Economics* 37 (1): 3–13.

Djankov, Simeon, Tim Ganser, Caralee McLiesh, Rita Ramalho, and Andrei Shleifer. 2010. "The Effect of Corporate Taxes on Investment and Entrepreneurship." *American Economic Journal: Macroeconomics* 2 (3): 31–64.

Djankov, Simeon, Dorina Georgieva, and Rita Ramalho. 2018. "Business Regulations and Poverty." *Economics Letters* 165 (April): 82–87.

Djankov, Simeon, Rafael La Porta, Florencio López-de-Silanes, and Andrei Shleifer. 2002. "The Regulation of Entry." *Quarterly Journal of Economics* 117 (1): 1–37.

Djankov, Simeon, Caralee McLiesh, and Rita Ramalho. 2006. "Regulation and Growth." *Economic Letters* 92 (3): 395–40.

Djankov, Simeon, Darshini Manraj, Caralee McLiesh, and Rita Ramalho. 2005. "Doing Business Indicators: Why Aggregate, and How to Do It." World Bank, Washington, DC.

Doblas-Madrid, Antonio, and Raoul Minetti. 2013. "Sharing Information in the Credit Market: Contract-Level Evidence from U.S. Firms." *Journal of Financial Economics* 109 (1): 198–223.

Dreher, Axel, and Martin Gassebner. 2013. "Greasing the Wheels? The Impact of Regulations and Corruption on Firm Entry." *Public Choice* 155 (3/4): 413–32.

Dudkin, Gerti, and Timo Välilä. 2006. "Transaction Costs in Public-Private Partnerships: A First Look at the Evidence." *Competition and Regulation in Network Industries* 7 (2): 307–31.

Esteller-Moré, Alejandro, Leonzio Rizzo, and Riccardo Secomandi. Forthcoming. "The Heterogenous Impact of Taxation on FDI: A Note on Djankov et al. (2010)." *Economics Letters.*

European Commission, DG Enterprise and Industry. 2014. "Evaluation of SMEs' Access to Public Procurement Markets in the EU: Final Report." European Commission, Brussels.

Fairlie, R., and A. Robb. 2009. "Gender Differences in Business Performance: Evidence from the Characteristics of Business Owners Survey." *Small Business Economics* 33 (4): 375–95.

Favara, Giovanni, Erwan Morellec, Enrique Schroth, and Philip Valta. 2017. "Debt Enforcement, Investment, and Risk-Taking Across Countries." *Journal of Financial Economics* 123 (1): 22–41.

Fernandes, Ana P., Priscila Ferreira, and L. Alan Winters. 2018. "The Effect of Competition on Executive Compensation and Incentives." *Journal of Human Resources* 53 (3): 783–824.

Fernández, Andrés, and César E. Tamayo. 2017. "From Institutions to Financial Development and Growth: What Are the Links?" *Journal of Economic Surveys* 31 (1): 17–57.

Flyvbjerg, Bent. 2017. "Introduction: The Iron Law of Megaproject Management." In *The Oxford Handbook of Megaproject Management,* edited by Bent Flyvbjerg, 1–18. Oxford, U.K.: Oxford University Press.

Flyvbjerg, Bent, Nils Bruzelius, and Werner Rothengatter. 2003. *Megaprojects and Risk: An Anatomy of Ambition.* Cambridge, U.K.: Cambridge University Press.

Flyvbjerg, Bent, Massimo Garbuio, and Dan Lovallo. 2009. "Delusion and Deception in Large Infrastructure Projects." *California Management Review* 51 (2): 170–93.

Francis, Bill B., Incheol Kim, Bin Wang, and Zhengyi Zhang. 2018. "Labor Law and Innovation Revisited." *Journal of Banking and Finance* 94 (September): 1–15.

Gaitho, Nancy Wanjiru. 2013. "Role of Credit Reference Bureaus on Credit Access in Kenya: A Survey of Commercial Banks in Kenya." *European Scientific Journal* 9 (13): 301–14.

Galletta, Sergio, Mario Jametti, and Agustin Redonda. 2015. "Highway to Economic Growth? Competition in Public Works Tenders in the Democratic Republic of Congo." *South African Journal of Economics* 83 (2): 240–52.

Gianfreda, Giuseppina, and Giovanna Vallanti. 2017. "Institutions' and Firms' Adjustments: Measuring the Impact of Courts' Delays on Job Flows and Productivity." *Journal of Law and Economics* 60 (1): 135–72.

Goldstein, Markus, Kenneth Houngbedji, Florence Kondylis, Michael O'Sullivan, and Harris Selod. 2018. "Formalization without Certification? Experimental Evidence on Property Rights and Investment." *Journal of Development Economics* 132 (May): 57–74.

Harju, Jarkko, Tuomas Matikka, and Timo Rauhanen. 2019. "Compliance Costs vs. Tax Incentives: Why Do Entrepreneurs Respond to Size-Based Regulations?" *Journal of Public Economics* 173 (May): 139–64.

Heckelman, Jac C. 2000. "Economic Freedom and Economic Growth: A Short-Run Causal Investigation." *Journal of Applied Economics* 3 (1): 71–91.

Herrendorf, Berthold, and Arilton Teixeira. 2011. "Barriers to Entry and Development." *International Economic Review* 52 (2): 573–602.

Hoffmann, Walther G., Franz Grumbach, and Helmut Hesse. 1965. *The Growth of the German Economy since the Mid-19th Century.* Berlin: Springer Verlag.

Hornok, Cecília, and Miklós Koren. 2015. "Administrative Barriers to Trade." *Journal of International Economics* 96 (S1): S110–22.

Houston, Joel F., Chen Lin, and Wensi Xie. 2018. "Shareholder Protection and the Cost of Capital." *Journal of Law and Economics* 61 (4): 677–710.

Ibrahim, Muazu, and Paul Alagidede. 2017. "Financial Development, Growth Volatility and Information Asymmetry in Sub-Saharan Africa: Does Law Matter?" *South African Journal of Economics* 85 (4): 570–88.

Iimi, Atsushi. 2006. "Auction Reforms for Effective Official Development Assistance." *Review of Industrial Organization* 28 (2): 109–28.

Jales, Hugo. 2018. "Estimating the Effects of the Minimum Wage in a Developing Country: A Density Discontinuity Design Approach." *Journal of Applied Econometrics* 33 (1): 29–51.

Jenwittayaroje, Nattawut, and Pornsit Jiraporn. 2019. "Do Independent Directors Improve Firm Value? Evidence from the Great Recession." *International Review of Finance* 19 (1): 207–22.

Karas, Alexei, William Pyle, and Koen Schoors. 2015. "A 'de Soto Effect' in Industry? Evidence from the Russian Federation." *Journal of Law and Economics* 58 (2): 451–80.

Kawaguchi, Daiji, and Tetsushi Murao. 2014. "Labor-Market Institutions and Long-Term Effects of Youth Unemployment." *Journal of Money, Credit and Banking* 46 (S2): 95–116.

Kenny, Charles. 2009. "Transport Construction, Corruption and Developing Countries." *Transport Reviews* 29 (1): 21–41.

Kinsey, Megan. 2004. "Transparency in Government Procurement: An International Consensus." *Public Contract Law Journal* 34 (1): 155.

Klapper, L., L. Laeven, and R. Rajan. 2006. "Entry Regulation as a Barrier to Entrepreneurship." *Journal of Financial Economics* 82 (3): 591–629.

Kleinknecht, Albert, Flore N. van Schaik, and Haibo Zhou. 2014. "Is Flexible Labour Good for Innovation? Evidence from Firm-Level Data." *Cambridge Journal of Economics* 38 (5): 1207–19.

Knack, Stephen, Nataliya Biletska, and Kanishka Kacker. 2017. "Deterring Kickbacks and Encouraging Entry in Public Procurement Markets: Evidence from Firm Surveys in 88 Developing Countries (English)." Policy Research Working Paper 8078, World Bank, Washington, DC.

Kraay, Aart, and Norikazu Tawara. 2013. "Can Specific Policy Indicators Identify Reform Priorities?" *Journal of Economic Growth* 18 (3): 253–83.

Kugler, Adriana D., and Gilles Saint-Paul. 2004. "How Do Firing Costs Affect Worker Flows in a World with Adverse Selection?" *Journal of Labor Economics* 22 (3): 553–84.

La Porta, Rafael, and Andrei Shleifer. 2008. "The Unofficial Economy and Economic Development." Tuck School of Business Working Paper 2009-57, Dartmouth College, Hanover, NH.

———. 2014. "Informality and Development." *Journal of Economic Perspectives* 28 (3): 109–26.

Lauer, Josh. 2017. *Creditworthy: A History of Consumer Surveillance and Financial Identity in America*. New York: Columbia University Press.

Lawless, Martina. 2013. "Do Complicated Tax Systems Prevent Foreign Direct Investment?" *Economica* 80 (317): 1–22.

Levine, Ross, Chen Lin, and Wensi Xie. 2016. "Spare Tire? Stock Markets, Banking Crises, and Economic Recoveries." *Journal of Financial Economics* 120 (1): 81–101.

Lichand, Guilherme, and Rodrigo R. Soares. 2014. "Access to Justice and Entrepreneurship: Evidence from Brazil's Special Civil Tribunals." *Journal of Law and Economics* 57 (2): 459–99.

Lisi, Domenico, and Miguel A. Malo. 2017. "The Impact of Temporary Employment on Productivity." *Journal for Labour Market Research* 50 (1): 91–112.

Madaus, Stephan. 2017. "The New Age of Debt and the Common Function of Insolvency and Restructuring Law." *Eurofenix* Spring: 14.

Marinescu, Ioana. 2009. "Job Security Legislation and Job Duration: Evidence from the United Kingdom." *Journal of Labor Economics* 27 (3): 465–86.

Martincus, Christian Volpe, Jerónimo Carballo, and Alejandro Graziano. 2015. "Customs." *Journal of International Economics* 96: 119–37.

Moyo, Busani. 2013. "Power Infrastructure Quality and Manufacturing Productivity in Africa: A Firm-Level Analysis." *Energy Policy* 61 (October): 1063–70.

Munemo, Jonathan. 2014. "Business Start-Up Regulations and the Complementarity between Foreign and Domestic Investment." *Review of World Economics* 150 (4): 745–61.

Muûls, Mirabelle. 2015. "Exporters, Importers and Credit Constraints." *Journal of International Economics* 95 (2): 333–43.

Onur, Ilke, Rasim Özcan, and Bedri Taş. 2012. "Public Procurement Auctions and Competition in Turkey." *Review of Industrial Organization* 40 (3): 207–23.

Ordoñez, Guillermo. 2013. "The Asymmetric Effects of Financial Frictions." *Journal of Political Economy* 121 (5): 844–95.

Pavel, Jan, and Eilia Sičáková-Beblavá. 2013. "Do E-Auctions Really Improve the Efficiency of Public Procurement? The Case of the Slovak Municipalities." *Prague Economic Papers* 2013 (1): 111–24.

Payne, Jennifer. 2013. "Debt Restructuring in English Law: Lessons from the US and the Need for Reform." University of Oxford Legal Research Series, Paper No. 89/2013, Oxford, U.K.

———. 2014. *Schemes of Arrangement: Theory, Structure and Operation.* Cambridge, U.K.: Cambridge University Press.

Pencavel, John. 2014. "The Productivity of Working Hours." Discussion Paper 8129, Institute of Labor Economics IZA, Bonn.

Ponticelli, Jacopo, and Leonardo S. Alencar. 2016. "Court Enforcement, Bank Loans, and Firm Investment: Evidence from a Bankruptcy Reform in Brazil." *Quarterly Journal of Economics* 131 (3): 1364–1413.

Ramalho, Rita, and Valentina Saltane. 2019. "Does Media Stimulate Reform Efforts?" Policy Research Working Paper 8984, World Bank, Washington, DC.

Rocha, Rudi, Gabriel Ulyssea, and Laísa Rachter. 2018. "Do Lower Taxes Reduce Informality? Evidence from Brazil." *Journal of Development Economics* 134 (September): 28–49.

Rose-Ackerman, Susan. 1996a. "The Political Economy of Corruption: Causes and Consequences." Viewpoint Note 74, World Bank, Washington, DC.

———. 1996b. "Redesigning the State to Fight Corruption." Viewpoint Note 75, World Bank, Washington, DC.

Schneider, Friedrich. 2005. "The Informal Sector in 145 Countries." Department of Economics, University of Linz, Austria.

Soraya, George. 2009. "Indonesian Experience Governance and Anticorruption Bali Urban Infrastructure Project (BUIP)," presentation to the World Bank GAC in Projects Group, April 21.

Tchamyou, Vanessa S., and Simplice A. Asongu. 2017. "Information Sharing and Financial Sector Development in Africa." *Journal of African Business* 18 (7): 24–49.

Vig, Vikrant. 2013. "Access to Collateral and Corporate Debt Structure: Evidence from a Natural Experiment." *Journal of Finance* 68 (3): 881–928.

Waseem, Mazhar. 2018. "Taxes, Informality and Income Shifting: Evidence from a Recent Pakistani Tax Reform." *Journal of Public Economics* 157 (January): 41–77.

Wells, Jill. 2013. "Corruption and Collusion in Construction: A View from the Industry." In *Corruption, Grabbing and Development,* edited by Tina Søreide and Aled Williams, 23–34. Northampton, U.K.: Edward Elgar Publishing.

World Bank. 2012. *Why Reform Public Procurement?* Washington, DC: World Bank.

———. 2018. *World Development Report 2019: The Changing Nature of Work.* Washington, DC: World Bank.

Yamada, Ken. 2016. "Tracing the Impact of Large Minimum Wage Changes on Household Welfare in Indonesia." *European Economic Review* 87 (August): 287–303.